GRADES 9-12

Mathematics
Assessment Sampler

Mathematics Assessment Sampler

A series edited by Anne M. Collins

GRADES 9-12

Mathematics Assessment Sampler

Items Aligned with NCTM's
Principles and Standards for School Mathematics

Betty Travis, *Editor*
University of Texas at San Antonio, San Antonio, Texas

Anne M. Collins, *Series Editor*
Boston College Mathematics Institute, Chestnut Hill, Massachusetts

WRITING TEAM
Terri Dahl
Jerry Johnson
Monique Morton
Sharon Walen

NCTM®

NATIONAL COUNCIL OF
TEACHERS OF MATHEMATICS

Library of Congress Cataloging-in-Publication Data

Mathematics assessment sampler, grades 9–12 : items aligned with NCTM's principles and standards for school mathematics / Betty Travis, editor ; writing team, Terri Dahl ...[et al.].
    p. cm. — (Mathematics assessment samplers)
  Includes bibliographical references.
  ISBN 0-87353-578-2
  1. Mathematics—Study and teaching (Secondary) 2. Mathematical ability—Testing. I. Travis, Betty. II. Dahl, Terri. III. Series.
  QA11.2.M2777 2005
  510'.71'2—dc22

                              2005022836

The National Council of Teachers of Mathematics is a public voice of mathematics education, providing vision, leadership, and professional development to support teachers in ensuring mathematics learning of the highest quality for all students.

PRINTED IN THE UNITED STATES OF AMERICA

Contents

On the Cover

The term *sampler* comes from the Latin *exemplum*, meaning "an example to be followed, a pattern, a model or example." The earliest known samplers date to the sixteenth century, although samplers were probably stitched long before that time. Beginning in the mid-eighteenth century, young girls commonly worked samplers as part of their education. During Victorian times, samplers metamorphosed into decorative articles hung by proud parents on parlor walls. As designs became more elaborate, generally only one stitch remained in use, leading to the well-known cross-stitch samplers of today.

The electronically "stitched" sampler on the cover highlights the relationships among knowledge (owl), learning (school), and the NCTM Standards (logo). The number patterns embedded in the border design (the counting sequence across the top; the Fibonacci sequence 1, 1, 2, 3, 5, 8, ... around the left, bottom, and right borders) echo pattern motifs seen in samplers in earlier times.

The Mathematics Assessment Samplers are intended to give teachers examples—not exhaustive listings—of assessment items that reveal what students know and can do in mathematics, that pinpoint areas of strengths and weakness in students' mathematical knowledge, and that shape teachers' curricular and instructional decisions toward the goal of maximizing all students' understanding of mathematics.

Preface

The National Council of Teachers of Mathematics asked our task force to compile a collection of assessment items that support *Principles and Standards for School Mathematics* (NCTM 2000). This book, one of four in the series, focuses on classroom assessment in grades 9–12. The other three books, for teachers in prekindergarten–grade 2, grades 3–5, and grades 6–8, also contain practical examples and samples of student work aligned with the NCTM Standards. Each of the books contains multiple-choice, short-response, and extended-response questions designed to help classroom teachers identify problems specifically related to certain of the NCTM Standards and Expectations. Matrices with this information are contained in the appendix.

NCTM's *Assessment Standards for School Mathematics* (1992) tells us that classroom assessment should—

- provide a rich variety of mathematical topics and problem situations;
- give students opportunities to investigate problems in many ways;
- question and listen to students;
- look for evidence of learning from many sources;
- expect students to use concepts and procedures effectively in solving problems.

Our collection of examples was compiled from many sources including state and provincial assessments. We know that standardized assessment has a major impact on what educators do in the classroom. Because most formal assessments include multiple-choice items, we have included them in this Sampler. Owing to the limited amount of information to be gleaned from most multiple-choice items, we have added an "explain your thinking," "justify your solution," or "how do you know?" component to most multiple-choice items. We believe that if students are going to be prepared to answer multiple-choice questions on formal assessments, they need classroom experience in answering this type of item, but we also want to be sure that students can support their answers by showing their work.

We have included a variety of rubrics as examples of how extended-response questions might be scored. We believe that students who know in advance how their answers will be evaluated will strive to meet the expected criteria; we realize, however, that for many assessment instruments, students are not privileged to this information. For classroom assessment, though, we believe that students should be given the rubric as a component of the assessment.

We encourage you to use these items with your students and hope that you find the bibliography and resources sections useful as you work toward extending your own classroom repertoire of assessment items.

Acknowledgments

The editors and writing team wish to thank the educators listed below for their suggestions, contributions of student work, reviews, and general assistance.

Barbara Bidlingmaier	Joyce Miller
Daniel Brahier	Lisa Mines
Elma Cadena	Sandy Norman
Bill Collins	Chad Olson
Terri Lynn Dahl	Joseph Ottum
Catherine Davis	Brad Packer
Linda Gann	Melissa Parma
Dennis Gittinger	Richard Schaeffer
Courtney Hall	Benjamin Rosario-Sosa
Elizabeth Hernandez	Diana Steele
Engried Johnson	Richard Travis
Julie Krueger	Barbara Uzzell
Aileen Mack	Amy Velasquez
Sherry Meier	Frances Basich-Whitney

The tasks from the Balanced Mathematics Assessment program (*Balanced Mathematics Assessment for the Mathematics Curriculum* [2002]; Schwartz and Kenney [2000]) were developed with the support of the National Science Foundation and the President Fellows of Harvard College.

The items from *Big Sky STARS: Student/Teacher Assessment Resources* were authored by Montana mathematics teachers and were published by the Montana Council of Teachers of Mathematics in 2003.

About This Series

An emphasis on assessment, testing, and gathering evidence of student achievement has become an educational phenomenon in recent years. In fact, we can fairly say that assessment is driving many educational decisions, including grade placement, graduation, and teacher evaluation. With that influence in mind, educators need to use good assessment material as a critical tool in the teaching and learning processes. Good problems are those that are mathematically rich, can be solved in multiple ways, promote critical thinking, and can be evaluated in a consistent manner—that is, teacher X and teacher Y would be likely to evaluate a problem in the same manner with the appropriate rubric.

Assessment is actually only one of three major considerations in the processes of teaching and learning. As such, assessment must be viewed in conjunction with curriculum and instruction. Just as a curriculum aligned with standards can guide instructional decisions, so too can assessment guide both instructional and curricular decisions. Therefore items designed to assess specific standards and expectations should be incorporated into the classroom repertoire of assessment tasks.

In its *Assessment Standards for School Mathematics* (*Assessment Standards*), the National Council of Teachers of Mathematics (NCTM 1995) articulated four purposes for assessments and their results: (1) monitoring students' progress toward learning goals, (2) making instructional decisions, (3) evaluating students' achievement, and (4) evaluating programs. Further, the Assessment Principle in *Principles and Standards for School Mathematics* (*Principles and Standards*) states that "assessment should not merely be done to students; rather it should be done for students" (NCTM 2000, p. 22). We have included a variety of rubrics in this series to assist the classroom teacher in providing feedback to students. Often, if students understand what is expected of them on individual extended-response problems, they tend to answer the questions more fully or provide greater detail than when they have no idea about the grading rubric being used.

This series was designed to present samples of student assessment items aligned with *Principles and Standards* (NCTM 2000). The items reflect the mathematics that all students should know and be able to do in grades prekindergarten–2, 3–5, 6–8, and 9–12. The items focus both on students' conceptual knowledge and on their procedural skills. The problems were designed as formative assessments—that is, assessments that help teachers learn how their students think about mathematical concepts, how students' understanding is communicated, and how such evidence can be used to guide instructional decisions.

The sample items contained in this publication are not a comprehensive set of examples but, rather, just a sampling. The problems are suitable for use as benchmark assessments or as evaluations of how well students have met particular NCTM Standards and

Expectations. Some student work is included with comments so that teachers can objectively examine a particular problem; study the way a student responded; and draw conclusions that, we hope, will translate into classroom practice.

This series also contains a chapter for professional development. This chapter was developed with preservice, in-service, and professional development staff in mind. It addresses the idea that by examining students' thinking, teachers can gain insight into what instruction is necessary to move students forward in developing mathematical proficiency. In other words, assessment can drive instructional decisions.

Assessment Standards (NCTM 1995) indicates that (a) assessment should enhance mathematics learning, (b) assessment should promote equity, (c) assessment should be an open process, (d) assessment should promote valid inferences about mathematics learning, and (e) assessment should be a coherent process. This series presents problems and tasks that, when used as one component of the assessment process, help meet those Assessment Standards.

Introduction: About This Book

THE PURPOSE of this book is to provide the classroom teacher with examples of assessment items for grades 9–12 that are aligned with the recommendations in *Principles and Standards for School Mathematics* (*Principles and Standards*) (NCTM 2000). Our intent is that this book will serve as a resource for teachers and teacher educators. We present sample problems that can be used to guide instruction and help teachers develop their own assessment items. The book is organized into six chapters—one for each of the content strands: Number and Operations, Algebra, Geometry, Measurement, and Data Analysis and Probability; and one on professional development for preservice and in-service teachers. The professional development chapter includes information on student errors and scoring rubrics.

The items are referenced with the Content Standards and Expectations outlined in *Principles and Standards* (NCTM 2000). Our goal is not to address every standard and expectation but only to furnish examples of Standards-based tasks that can be incorporated into mathematics instruction. Some items address two content areas and are listed in both chapters. The Process Standards: Problem Solving, Reasoning and Proof, Communication, Connections, and Representation, are indicated in the item matrices in the appendix. The items are not intended to be used as test problems for scoring or grading. They are designed for classroom use as a collection of exemplar assessment items that teachers can use to guide their instruction.

Item Sources

The items included here have been selected or modified from various sources, including—

- the Third International Mathematics and Science Study (TIMSS);
- the National Assessment of Educational Progress (NAEP);
- *Balanced Assessment for the 21st Century* (Schwartz and Kenney 2000);
- *Montana Mathematics Assessment Handbook;*
- Great Falls Public Schools;
- Massachusetts Department of Education;
- Oregon Department of Education;
- Mathematical Association of America;
- Programme for International Student Assessment (PISA);
- Charles Dana Center at the University of Texas at Austin; and
- NCTM's *Principles and Standards for School Mathematics* (2000).

as well as selected textbook problems. Other items were written or have been used by committee members who are classroom teachers and mathematics educators. Although we have made every effort to acknowledge item sources, a few problems are from unknown sources.

Item Types

The item types included here are multiple choice, short response, and extended response. Multiple-choice questions are included for several reasons. These items can be used to diagnose certain types of errors by carefully constructing distractors that address students' misunderstandings. Since most state and national tests use multiple-choice questions, their use lets students familiarize themselves with the item format and the strategies that they can use in answering this type of question.

Without students' work, answers do not adequately inform teachers about what students do and do not know. Just examining multiple-choice answers as being right or wrong provides little information to guide instructional decisions. A correct answer may indicate a lucky guess or an understanding of the mathematics; we do not know which. Therefore, all multiple-choice items included here either require students to explain their answers or ask comparative questions among answer choices.

Short-response and extended-response items help students develop their mathematical communication skills by explaining answers and writing solutions. This requirement forces them to think about what they did and why. Some problems are "scaffolded" problems, building up in mathematical difficulty so that every student has entry into the problem. We wish to emphasize that assessment can be accomplished in many ways. The question formats we use here constitute only one form of assessment. Portfolios, observations, interviews with students, journals, student projects, and presentations are equally valid forms of assessment and can provide extremely useful information that together present a coherent and complete picture with which to evaluate student learning and guide instruction.

Student Work

In each chapter, the reader will see selected samples of student work, some having correct solutions and others exhibiting certain types of errors. Most of the errors fall into four general categories: miscommunicating understanding, communicating a misunderstanding, evidencing mistakes in basic arithmetic or algebraic skills, and misreading the problem. More about these types of errors can be found in the work of Bright and Joyner (2004). We include examples of the foregoing error types throughout each chapter to illustrate our error-classification scheme. We present more extensive explanations with additional student work in the chapter on professional development, which also includes information on scoring and using rubrics to help analyze students' levels of understanding.

Technology

Most of the items included here can be worked without using a calculator. We intend that the calculator be used only to assist students with their thought processes and as a helpful tool, not as a crutch to mask their misunderstandings or lack of knowledge. We include a few problems for which calculators should not be used, for the reason that their use would hinder students in solving the problem. We also include a few problems that require the use of a calculator—either as a tool for approximating sine values and logarithms or for graphing lines in an exercise involving successive approximations for line-of-sight equations.

Professional Development

We close with a chapter on professional development to help in-service and preservice teachers examine student work and assess student errors. By looking at student work, teachers can get a clearer picture of what students perceive about the mathematics they are asked to do. When students are asked to explain their reasoning or justify their responses, the assessment assumes a more informative role than when the correct answer is the only focus. The guiding principle for assessment is that an item must help in answering the question "What is the evidence that students are learning?" Does a piece of student work furnish objective evidence that the student understands the mathematics in question? That the student lacks understanding of the mathematics in question? Or, often, that the student has some level of understanding, together with some misconceptions? Teachers who examine students' work in terms of both the mathematics content and the solution processes reflected in specific items are then better equipped to identify strengths and weaknesses that can be used to determine appropriate next steps for instruction.

The chapter also discusses scoring rubrics that can be used to evaluate students' work. The rubric may be holistic and look at the overall quality of the students' performance, or it may be analytic and look at different components. Samples of both types of scoring schemes, along with explanations and guidelines, are included in the chapter.

Conclusion

In producing this compilation of assessment items, we hope to offer teachers a classroom-assessment framework that presents exemplary assessment items and suggests how assessment might be used to shape instructional practice. Our goal is to provide a model process and appropriate resources that teachers can adopt and adapt for classroom use. We wish to guide educators in developing assessment items that teachers can use as a basis for instructional changes in the classroom.

Number and Operations

ASSESSMENT items in this chapter are samples designed to exemplify the Process Standards and student Expectations for Number and Operations as outlined in *Principles and Standards for School Mathematics* (NCTM 2000). The goal is to present items that go beyond algorithmic manipulation and that delve more deeply into numbers and their operations. High school students need to use variables and functions to represent relationships among sets of numbers, look at properties of classes of numbers, and understand number systems and their structures. Specific items in this chapter assess students' proficiency with factorials and exponential representations of large numbers, students' reasoning with rational and irrational numbers, and their knowledge of counting techniques. The chapter ends with two "challenger" problems involving Mersenne primes, infinite sequences, and measures of infinite sets.

The problem types include two multiple choice, five short response, and two extended response, incorporating the Process Standards of Problem Solving, Reasoning and Proof, Communication, Connections, and Representations.

Some student work is included in this chapter, either exemplifying good solution techniques and thinking strategies or containing commonly made mistakes that demonstrate a lack of understanding, an inability to communicate mathematically, or errors in basic skills.

Number and Operations Assessment Items

Standard: Understand numbers, ways of representing numbers, relationships among numbers, and number systems

Expectation: Develop a deeper understanding of very large and very small numbers and of various representations of them

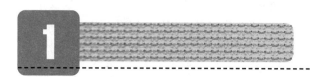

List these numbers in increasing order: 2^{800}, 3^{600}, 5^{400}, 6^{200}

Smallest	_____
Second	_____
Third	_____
Largest	_____

How did you decide?

> **About the mathematics:** This item can be used to determine students' understandings of and abilities to apply mathematical processes in situations involving exponential representation of very large numbers. It helps students develop a sense of the magnitude of large numbers and a strategy for decomposing them. It also allows students to organize and consolidate their mathematical thinking by explaining their solutions.
>
> **Solution:** 6^{200}, 2^{800}, 5^{400}, 3^{600}
>
> $$2^{800} = (2^4)^{200} \qquad 3^{600} = (3^3)^{200} \qquad 5^{400} = (5^2)^{200} \qquad 6^{200}$$
> $$\quad = 16^{200} \qquad\qquad = 27^{200} \qquad\qquad = 25^{200} \qquad = 6^{200}$$
>
> $$6^{200} < 16^{200} < 25^{200} < 27^{200}$$
> $$6^{200} < 2^{800} < 5^{400} < 3^{600}$$

Student Work

Student A

This student understands that when the exponents are the same, the bases can be compared to determine order.

List these numbers in increasing order: $2^{800}, 3^{600}, 5^{400}, 6^{200}$

Smallest 6^{200}

Second 2^{800}

Third 5^{400}

Largest 3^{600}

How did you decide?

$$2^{800} = \left(2^8\right)^{100} = 256^{100}$$

$$3^{600} = \left(3^6\right)^{100} = 729^{100}$$

$$5^{400} = \left(5^4\right)^{100} = 625^{100}$$

$$6^{200} = \left(6^2\right)^{100} = 36^{100}$$

Student B

The error made by this student was common throughout students' work. They assumed that the largest exponent produces the largest number, regardless of the base.

Smallest 6^{200}

Second 5^{400}

Third 3^{600}

Largest 2^{800}

How did you decide?

Though the base number is larger, the true value is based on the exponents, so the largest value of exponent will be the largest number.

Standard: Understand numbers, ways of representing numbers, relationships among numbers, and number systems

Expectation: Develop a deeper understanding of very large and very small numbers and of various representations of them

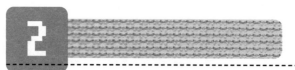

What is the units digit of 3^{1992}? Write a convincing mathematical argument that supports your solution.

About the mathematics: This item can be used to illustrate for students what is expected in a convincing mathematical argument. It also allows teachers to identify students' misunderstandings about the basic properties of exponents (see student B's work).

Solution: 1

Because 1992 is divisible by 4, we can write

$$3^{1992} = (3^4)^{498}$$
$$= (81)^{498},$$

which must end in 1.

Student Work

Student A

This student made a table to recognize the pattern and knew that when the exponent is divided by 4, the remainder determines the units digit.

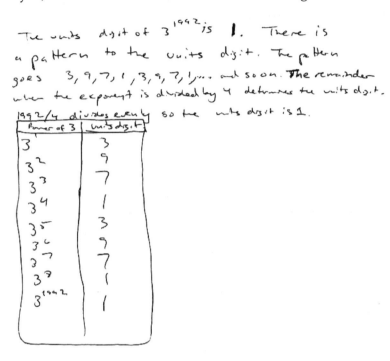

The units digit of 3^{1992} is **1**. There is a pattern to the units digit. The pattern goes 3, 9, 7, 1, 3, 9, 7, 1,... and so on. **The remainder** when the exponent is divided by 4 determines the units digit. 1992/4 divides evenly so the units digit is 1.

Power of 3	Units digit
3	3
3^2	9
3^3	7
3^4	1
3^5	3
3^6	9
3^7	7
3^8	1
3^{1992}	1

Student B

Student B based his work on a very common error (in step 2), which represents a serious misconception about exponents. He also was so determined to use a calculator that he lost sight of what he needed to do to answer the problem.

$3^{(996+996)}$

$3^{996} + 3^{996}$

$3^{(19}$

$3^{(124.5)}(124.5)(124.5)$ $3^{124.5} + 3^{124.5} + 3^{124.5} + 3^{124.5} + 3^{124.5} + 3^{124.5} + 3^{124.5} +$

$3^{124.5} + 3^{124.5} + 3^{124.5} + 3^{124.5} + 3^{124.5} + 3^{124.5} + 3^{124.5} + 3^{124.5}$

2.52×10^{59}

$\times \quad 16$

$3^{1992} = \boxed{4.03 \times 10^{60}}$

Standard: Understand numbers, ways of representing numbers, relationships among numbers, and number systems

Expectation: Develop a deeper understanding of very large and very small numbers and of various representations of them

Given the expression $1! + 2! + \cdots + 205!$, what is the units digit of the sum? Clearly communicate your reasoning, and explain how you know that your response is mathematically correct.

About the mathematics: This item is a good example of finding patterns to solve problems. It also makes use of the problem-solving strategy of breaking down problems into smaller parts. It also allows students to make and investigate mathematical conjectures and to communicate their mathematical reasoning.

Solution: 3

$$1! = 1$$
$$1! + 2! = 3$$
$$1! + 2! + 3! = 9$$
$$1! + 2! + 3! + 4! = 33$$
$$1! + 2! + 3! + 4! + 5! = 153$$
$$1! + 2! + 3! + 4! + 5! + 6! = 873$$

Note: $5! = 1 \times 2 \times 3 \times 4 \times 5 = 12 \times 10 = 120$. All factorials higher than 4! contain 2×5 as part of the product. Therefore, the units digit for all factorials higher than 4! will be 0. The units digit of the sum does not change after adding the fourth factorial, so the units digit remains 3.

Student Work

Student A

Although the answer is correct, the student made a mistake calculating 2! and 3!.

$$1! = 1 \quad 2! = 3 \quad 3! = 9 \quad 4! = 24 \quad 5! = 120 \quad 6! = 720 \quad 7! = 5040 \quad 8! = 40320$$

The units digit of the sum $1! + 2! + \ldots + 206!$ is 3. $1! + \ldots + 4! = \mathbf{33}$ ends in a three. All factorials after 4 end in zero. The unit digit of 33 plus a string of numbers that end in zero will always be three.

Student B

Student B relied too much on formulas. This student lost sight of the question being asked.

~~1 + 2 + 6 + 24 + 120 +~~

$$\sum_{n=1}^{205} ($$

There is an easier way to do this problem however I have forgotten the formula. So here is the extremely long and tedious way of solving the problem.

$1 + 2 + 6 + 24 + 120 + 720 + 5040 + 40320 + 362880 + \underset{3991680}{\cancel{3628800}} + 479001600 + 6227020800$

$87178291200 + 1.3077E12 + 2.0923E13 + 3.5569E14 + 6.4024E15 + 1.2465E17 + 2.4329E18 + 5.1091E19 +$

$1.1240E21 + 2.5852E22 + 6.2045E23 + 1.5511E25) \times 8.2$

$1.6158E25 +$

$4.1944E26 (8.2) = 3.4394E27$

roughly $\approx 3.4394E27$

a very huge #

This is correct I believe because I used ! to find the total sum, however it would have been much easier with the formula.

Standard: Understand meanings of operations and how they relate to one another

Expectation: Judge the effects of such operations as multiplication, division, and computing powers and roots on the magnitudes of quantities

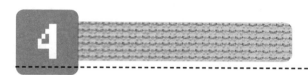

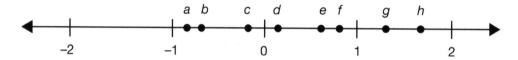

Given the points with coordinates $a, b, c, \ldots, h$ as shown, which point is closest to—

a. ab?

b. $|c|$?

c. $1/f$?

d. $\sqrt{e}$?

e. $\sqrt{h}$?

Source: Adapted from *Principles and Standards for School Mathematics* (NCTM 2000, p. 293, fig. 7.1)

About the mathematics: This problem involves estimation, number sense, and reasoning with rational and irrational numbers. This reasoning is important as students learn to judge the reasonableness of their answers. Students can select and use various types of reasoning and methods of solution.

Solution

a. The value of ab must be positive because a and b are negative.

The value of ab must be less than 1 because a and b are between –1 and 0.

The value of ab will not be greater than $|a|$ because we are taking a fraction of a fraction.

Point e appears to be closest to the value of ab.

b. Point *d* appears to be closest to the value of |*c*| because *c* and *d* are approximately the same distance from zero.

c. Point *g* appears to be closest to the value of $^1/_f$ because *f* is less than 1 but close to 1. Therefore $^1/_f$ must be greater than 1 but closer to 1.

d. Point *f* appears to be closest to the value of $\sqrt{e}$ because the square root of a number between 0 and 1 is also between 0 and 1, yet larger than the number.

e. Point *g* appears to be closest to the value of $\sqrt{h}$ because the square root of a number between 1 and 2 is also between 1 and 2, yet smaller than the number.

Student Work

Student A

The method of assigning approximate values is a common strategy used by students. This student used a combination of assigning values to these points and listing some number properties to answer the questions.

a) • e would be the closest estimate to ab because a negative multiplied by a negative is a positive. • a is approximately $-5/6$ and • b is approximately $-2/3$. $-5/6 (-2/3) = 5/9$ and e looks closest to $5/9$.

b) • d would be closest to |c| because |c| is going to be a positive version of •c.

c) • g would be the closest to $1/f$ because $1/f$ is the same as 1 times the reciprocal of f. •F is approximately $5/6$ and $1 \cdot 6/5 = 6/5$ or approximately •g.

d) • f would be the closest to $\sqrt{e}$. • e is approximately $2/3$ and $\sqrt{2/3} \approx 0.82$ making •f the closest estimate.

e) • g would be the closest estimate to $\sqrt{h}$. •h is approximately $15/6$ and $\sqrt{15/6} \approx 1.35$ making •g the closest estimate.

Student B

This student's approach of substituting approximate values is satisfactory but does not use number properties that can be generalized. The student also failed to answer the questions and chose inappropriate values for some of the points.

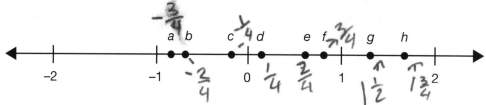

Given the points with coordinates $a, b, c, \ldots, h$ as shown, which point is closest to—

a. ab? $+\dfrac{3}{4} \cdot -\dfrac{1}{4}$ $\dfrac{6}{16} = \boxed{\dfrac{3}{4}}$

b. $|c|$? $\left|-\dfrac{1}{4}\right|$ $\boxed{\dfrac{1}{4}}$

c. $1/f$? $\dfrac{1}{\tfrac{3}{4}}$

d. $\sqrt{e}$? $\sqrt{\tfrac{1}{2}}$

e. $\sqrt{h}$? $\sqrt{\tfrac{3}{4}}$

Standard: Understand meanings of operations and how they relate to one another

Expectation: Judge the effects of such operations as multiplication, division, and computing powers and roots on the magnitudes of quantities

5

An examination consists of thirteen questions. A student must answer only one of the first two questions and only nine of the remaining ones. How many choices of questions does the student have?

a. $_{13}C_{10} = 286$
b. $_{11}C_8 = 165$
c. $2 \times {}_{11}C_9 = 110$
d. $2 \times {}_{11}P_2 = 220$
e. none of the above

Source: TIMSS Population 3 Item Pool (L-4)

About the mathematics: This problem can help us understand students' misconceptions about combinations and permutations. It also allows us to help students understand the difference between "how many ways" and probability.

Solution: c

One of the first two questions: $_2C_1$

Nine of the remaining eleven questions: $_{11}C_9$

$_2C_1 \times {}_{11}C_9$ or $2 \times {}_{11}C_9$ (because $_2C_1 = \dfrac{2!}{1!1!} = 2$)

$$2 \times \frac{11!}{2!9!} = 2 \times 55 = 110$$

Student Work

Student A

This student did an excellent job of solving the problem and showing all her work. She realized that 2 is equivalent to $_2C_1$.

a. $_{13}C_{10} = 286$

b. $_{11}C_8 = 165$

c. $2 \times {}_{11}C_9 = 110$

d. $2 \times {}_{11}P_2 = 220$

e. none of the above

$_2C_1 \cdot {}_{11}C_9$

$\dfrac{2!}{1!1!} \cdot {}_{11}C_9$

$2 \cdot \dfrac{11!}{2!9!} = 110$

Student B

Student B, despite showing an understanding of the problem, chose an incorrect distractor, possibly because she did not understand that

$$_2C_1 = \frac{2!}{1!1!} = 2.$$

a. $_{13}C_{10} = 286$

b. $_{11}C_8 = 165$

c. $2 \times {}_{11}C_9 = 110$

d. $2 \times {}_{11}P_2 = 220$

e. none of the above → the answer is 110 different ways.

$2C_1 \cdot {}_{11}C_9 = 110$

Student C

Student C knew some combination procedures but did not know how or when to use them.

a. $_{13}C_{10} = 286$

b. $_{11}C_8 = 165$

c. $2 \times {}_{11}C_9 = 110$

d. $2 \times {}_{11}P_2 = 220$

e. none of the above

$\dfrac{_2C_1 \cdot {}_{11}C_9}{_{13}C_{10}} = \dfrac{\overset{11}{36788}}{286} = \dfrac{11}{107.783368}$

$_{13}C_{10} = 286$

Standard: Understand meanings of operations and how they relate to one another

Expectation: Develop an understanding of permutations and combinations as counting techniques

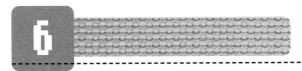

In how many ways can one arrange on a bookshelf 5 thick books, 4 medium-sized books, and 3 thin books so that the books of the same size remain together?

a. 5! 4! 3! 3! = 103,680
b. 5! 4! 3! = 17,280
c. (5! 4! 3!) × 3 = 51,840
d. 5 × 4 × 3 × 3 = 180
e. 2^{12} × 3 = 12,288

Source: TIMSS Population 3 Item Pool (K-2)

About the mathematics: This problem allows teachers to determine whether students are able to show their understanding of arrangements when different groups—thick, medium, and thin—are present within the total arrangement. Students must realize that the groups can also be arranged; this aspect increases the difficulty of the problem.

Solution: a

The number of ways to arrange the thick, medium, and thin groups is 3 × 2 × 1. So the total number of ways to arrange the twelve books is 5! 4! 3! 3!, or 103,680.

Student Work

Student A

This student's work shows a complete understanding of the problem.

    a. 5! 4! 3! 3! = 103 680

    b. 5! 4! 3! = 17 280

    c. (5! 4! 3!) x 3 = 51 840

    d. 5 x 4 x 3 x 3 = 180

    e. 2^{12} x 3 = 12 288

arrange 5 books = 5!

arrange 4 books = 4!

arrange 3 books = 3!

The books have to stay together so the sets are like one big book and there's three of them. So you can arrange these in another 3! ways.

Multiply all together

Student B

Student B made the most common error seen throughout students' work. This student and many others neglected to consider the order of the size of the books.

For the group of 5, the first book can be any of the five, the second can be any of the remaining four, the third can be any of the remaining three, and so on... this can be found by: 5! * 4! * 3! = 17280

(5 x 4 x 3 x 2 x 1)

Standard: Understand meanings of operations and how they relate to one another

Expectation: Develop an understanding of permutations and combinations as counting techniques

7

While working on a problem, Christine observed that $_5P_1$ and $_5C_1$ give the same value but that the value for $_5P_2$ is larger than the value for $_5C_2$. Explain why this outcome occurs.

> **Source:** Adapted from Nova Scotia Department of Education (2002)
> **About the mathematics:** This problem requires students to understand the differences between permutations and combinations. It also helps students understand how basic statistical techniques are written and evaluated.
> **Solution**

$$_5P_1 = \frac{5!}{(5-1)!} = \frac{5!}{4!} \qquad\qquad _5C_1 = \frac{5!}{1!(5-1)!} = \frac{5!}{1!4!}$$

$$_5P_2 = \frac{5!}{(5-2)!} = \frac{5!}{3!} \qquad\qquad _5C_2 = \frac{5!}{2!(5-2)!} = \frac{5!}{2!3!}$$

Standard: Understand numbers, ways of representing numbers, relationships among numbers, and number systems

Expectation: Compare and contrast the properties of numbers and number systems, including the rational and real numbers

Challenger

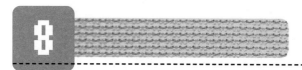

You are the Keeper of the Digits 0, 1, 2, 3, 4, 5, 6, 7, 8, and 9. On the way to school this morning, you lost the digit 9. What happens to our base ten number line as a result of the loss of the digit 9?

Source: Unknown

About the mathematics: This task gives students the opportunity to explore the concept of numbers along a number line. They need to have familiarity with the sum of an infinite sequence and be able to interpret that sum. We recommend that the problem be presented in parts, culminating with an informal discussion of sets with measure zero and sets with measure one. This approach will stretch students' understanding of our number system and can lead to discussions of other sets with these characteristics. This problem should be challenging and fun for your advanced students.

Solution: Rather than look at the entire number line, examine what happens on the interval [0, 1].

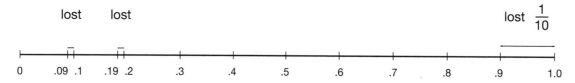

The length of the interval is 1. Remove all the numbers in [0.9, 1) because they all contain the digit 9. Next work through each of the subintervals: [0, 0.1), [0.1, 0.2), ... , [0.8, 0.9). Everything is lost in the following subintervals: [0.09, 0.1), [0.19, 0.2), ... , [0.89, 0.9). Continue in this same manner for [0.009, 0.01).

The loss of 9 as a first digit removes

$$\frac{1}{10}$$

of the interval from [0, 1]. The loss of 9 as a second digit removes

$$\frac{9}{100}$$

of the interval. The loss of 9 as a third digit removes

$$\frac{81}{1000}$$

of the interval. The loss of 9 as an nth digit removes

$$\frac{1}{10}\left(\frac{9}{10}\right)^{n-1}$$

of the interval.

Calculate the losses:

$$\frac{1}{10}+\frac{9}{10^2}+\frac{9^2}{10^3}+\cdots+\frac{9^{n-1}}{10^n}+\cdots$$

$$S=\frac{\frac{1}{10}}{1-\frac{9}{10}}=1$$

The interval from 0 to 1 is lost! The same can be done with the interval (1, 2] and all other intervals. What remains is a set of measure zero. The number line collapses. A lot of numbers remain (e.g., many of the endpoints and even many irrationals, such as 0.010010001000010000010000001...), but the set of all numbers that do not have the digit 9 in their decimal representation has measure zero and could not fill a continuous interval, no matter how small.

21

Standard: Understand numbers, ways of representing numbers, relationships among numbers, and number systems

Expectation: Develop a deeper understanding of very large and very small numbers and of various representations of them

Challenger

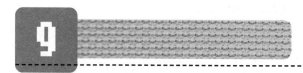

Mersenne primes are of the special form

$$M_p = 2^p - 1,$$

where p is another prime. (Not all values of p give primes. $M_2 = 3$, $M_3 = 7$, $M_5 = 31$, $M_7 = 127$, but $M_{11} = 2047$, which is not prime.) How many digits are in the Mersenne prime $M_{24,036,583}$?

About the mathematics: This item assesses whether students can use their knowledge of primes as well as understand the algebraic expression used for this special type of prime. The problem should be presented with guidance and discussion on how to determine the size of numbers. This problem presents a good opportunity to bring in students' knowledge of the parts of a logarithm (characteristic and mantissa) and what each part tells us.

Teacher note: Students can participate in a worldwide research project called the Great Internet Mersenne Prime Search (GIMPS). The project is part of an international grid of more than 205,000 interconnected computers operated by Entropia, Incorporated. GIMPS was formed in January 1996 by George Woltman to discover new Mersenne primes. GIMPS harnesses the power of hundreds of thousands of small computers to search for these numbers. Anyone with a reasonably powerful computer can join the search by downloading the free software from www.mersenne.org/prime.htm.

Solution

Instead of finding the number of digits in $M_p = 2^p - 1$, we will find the number of digits in $M_p + 1 = 2^p$. These two numbers have the same number of digits, because if $M_p + 1$ had one more digit, it would have to end in 0. But because it equals 2^p, it will end only in 2, 4, 6, or 8. To find the number of digits in $2^{24,036,583}$, we can use logarithms:

$$\log 2^{24,036,583} = 24{,}036{,}583(\log 2) \approx 7235732.6$$

Because the characteristic of the logarithm is 7235732, we conclude that the number $2^{24,036,583}$ has 7,235,733 digits (since the characteristic indicates the number of decimal places of a number in scientific notation).

Algebra

STANDARDS-based problems that exemplify the Algebra Standards for school mathematics (NCTM 2000) constitute the items in this chapter. These problems emphasize relationships among quantities, ways of representing functions, and the analysis of change. They focus on helping students understand patterns and functions, analyze mathematical situations and structures, interpret change, and use mathematical models to solve problems. They require students to generate functions, understand relationships between graphical and algebraic representations, and analyze different classes of functions, such as step, periodic, and exponential.

Eighteen problems are included, three of which are multiple choice, nine are short response, and six are extended response. Several of the extended-response problems use *scaffolding*, a technique enabling all students' entry into a problem by gradually building the difficulty level. Scaffolding also allows for mathematically rich problems. Most items address two or more of the Process Standards of Problem Solving, Reasoning and Proof, Communication, Connections, and Representation (NCTM 2000). The matrix in the appendix correlates each problem with the specific Content and Process Standards and student Expectations for Algebra.

The chapter also includes samples of student work demonstrating correct solutions and strategies or evidencing errors commonly made by students.

Algebra Assessment Items

Standard: Use mathematical models to represent and understand quantitative relationships

Expectations: (a) Identify essential quantitative relationships in a situation and determine the class or classes of functions that might model the relationship; (b) draw reasonable conclusions about a situation being modeled

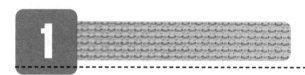

The price of a particular product doubles every 35 years. If the price of the product was $16.50 on January 1, 1996, then the price of the product will be $36.50 in what year?

a. 2028
b. 2031
c. 2036
d. 2040

Justify your answer.

> **Source:** Adapted from Nova Scotia Department of Education (2002)
> **About the mathematics:** This item assesses whether students understand how to write and use a mathematical expression for doubling. Although it can be solved graphically on a calculator using lists and regression, no student in our pilot sample used a doubling equation.

Solution: c

$$y = 16.50 \cdot 2^x$$

$$36.50 = 16.50 \cdot 2^x$$

$$2^x = \frac{36.50}{16.50} \approx 2.21$$

$$x = \frac{\log 2.21}{\log 2} \approx 1.144$$

$$35(1.144) \approx 40$$

$$1996 + 40 = 2036$$

Student Work

Student A

This student determined that in the year 2031, the product would have doubled in price. The reasoning that the student used in applying a strategy is difficult to follow. If the student had labeled his work, his thinking would have been easier to discern. The work shown does not appear to give an answer to the question asked.

Student B

This student set up a proportion to get her answer. If the student had labeled all her work, her reasoning would have been easier to follow. Her work does not appear to lead to an answer to the question asked.

Standard: Represent and analyze mathematical situations and structures using algebraic symbols

Expectation: Understand the meaning of equivalent forms of expressions, equations, inequalities, and relations

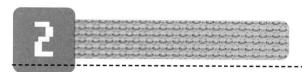

If $xy = 1$ and x is greater than 0, which of the following statements is true? Show the work that justifies your answer.

a. When x is greater than 1, y is negative.
b. When x is greater than 1, y is greater than 1.
c. When x is less than 1, y is less than 1.
d. As x increases, y increases.
e. As x increases, y decreases.

> **Source:** TIMSS Population 3 Item Pool (K-1)
> **About the mathematics:** This problem can be solved graphically, algebraically, or numerically and shows relationships between numbers. It also allows students to make and justify mathematical conjectures.

Solution: e

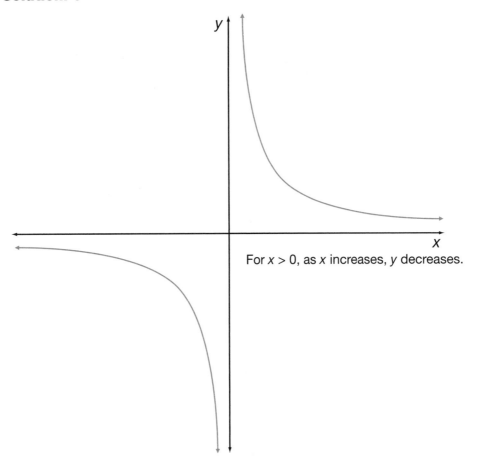

For $x > 0$, as x increases, y decreases.

Or the problem could be solved by examining several ordered pairs where x is greater than 1 and is increasing or x is less than 1:

$$\left(2, \frac{1}{2}\right), \left(3, \frac{1}{3}\right), \left(\frac{1}{2}, 2\right), \left(\frac{1}{3}, 3\right)$$

Although this method may help eliminate some answer possibilities, it does not prove that the answer is e.

Student Work

Student A

This student used counterexamples to eliminate all answers except choice e. But he needs to be careful about his reasoning as to why statement e is true. Four examples do not prove the statement. Only through his process of eliminating all other choices did he choose answer e.

$$xy = 1$$

a. $2(-1) = -1 \quad xy \neq 1 \quad \text{False}$

b. $2(2) = 4 \quad xy \neq 1 \quad \text{false}$

c. $.9(.9) = .81 \\ .5(.5) = .25 \quad xy \neq 1 \quad \text{false}$

d. $(1)1 = 1 \\ 2(2) = 4 \quad \text{false} \\ 3(3) = 9$

e. $1(1) = 1. \\ 2(\frac{1}{2}) = 1 \\ 3(\frac{1}{3}) = 1 \quad \text{True} \\ 4(\frac{1}{4}) = 1$

E is the only true statement.

Student B

This student got the right answer, but some of the statements he used to eliminate some choices are not correct. This example illustrates the importance of requiring students to explain their work, especially with multiple-choice items.

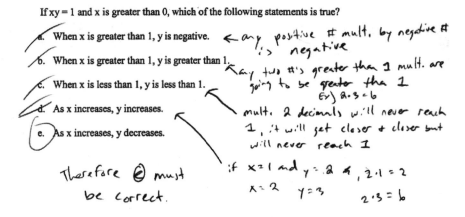

If $xy = 1$ and x is greater than 0, which of the following statements is true?

a. When x is greater than 1, y is negative. ← any positive # mult. by negative # is negative

b. When x is greater than 1, y is greater than 1. ← any two #'s greater than 1 mult. are going to be greater than 1 Ex) 2·3 = 6

c. When x is less than 1, y is less than 1. ← mult. 2 decimals will never reach 1, it will get closer & closer but will never reach 1

d. As x increases, y increases.

e. As x increases, y decreases.

Therefore e must be correct.

if $x = 1$ and $y = 2$ ∴ $2 \cdot 1 = 2$
$x = 2 \quad y = 3 \quad 2 \cdot 3 = 6$

Standard: Use mathematical models to represent and understand quantitative relationships

Expectation: Identify essential quantitative relationships in a situation and determine the class or classes of functions that might model the relationships

3

In February 2000 the cost of sending a letter by first-class mail was 33 cents for the first ounce and an additional 22 cents for each additional ounce or portion thereof through 13 ounces. Choose the graph that best represents the cost of mailing a letter that weighs 4 ounces or less.

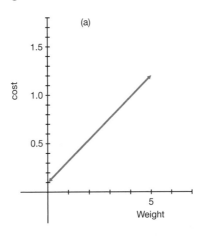

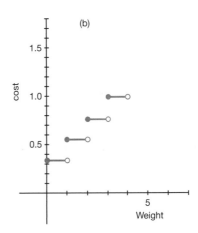

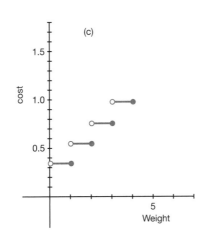

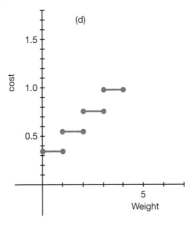

Source: Adapted from *Principles and Standards for School Mathematics* (NCTM 2000, p. 298, fig. 7.4)

About the mathematics: This item allows students to use graphical data to analyze, interpret, and understand a special function. Class discussion as to why the answer is a step function is important in helping students understand various classes of functions.

Solution: c

Student Work

Student A

Student A answered correctly and referenced the open versus closed endpoints. However, she did not explain the difference between the open and closed endpoints.

> C because the 33 ¢ counts through the 1st ounce but once you past the 1st ounce you have 33¢ plus 22 ¢ so that's why you have closed dots at the end of your step and open at the beginning.

Student B

Student B answered correctly and used a process-of-elimination method. This student justified reasons for eliminating distractors a and d. The student explained the interpretation of the open endpoint in reference to having a package with no weight.

> Graph (a) cannot express this relationship – as you cannot have a negative weight, as seen in the graph. Likewise graph (d) cannot be correct since it isn't a function, so if you had 2 ounces, would you pay 55 or 77 cents? So the answer must be either (b) or (c). My guess is C, since it has an open circle on the y-axis, meaning if you had a zero weight package, you'd pay nothing. As graph (b) suggests, if you weren't sending anything at all, why would you have to pay? C is the most logical, as you get to the first ounce, you pay 33 ¢, then immediately after you rise up to the second "stairstep."

Student C

Student C answered incorrectly and made a vague reference to the fact that the cost changes by the ounce. This student did not effectively justify his answer.

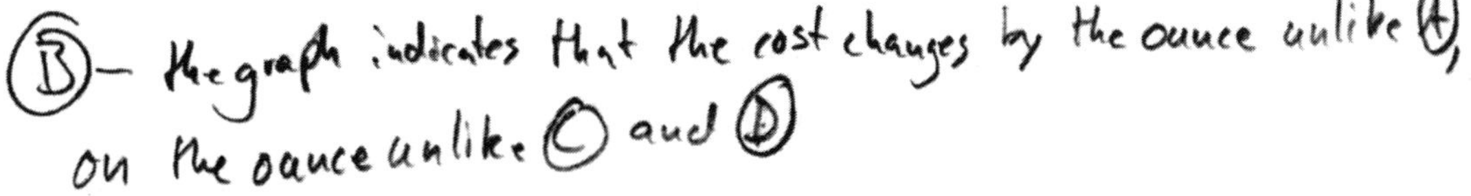

(B)— the graph indicates that the cost changes by the ounce unlike (A), on the ounce unlike (C) and (D)

Student D

Student D answered incorrectly. He appears to have misunderstood the idea of open and closed endpoints, since graph b gives $0.77 for a 2-ounce letter rather than the $0.55 that he stated it would cost.

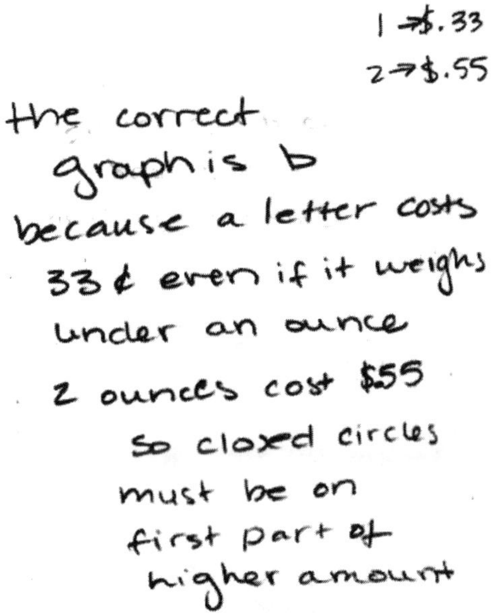

1 → $.33
2 → $.55

the correct
graph is b
because a letter costs
33¢ even if it weighs
under an ounce

2 ounces cost $55
so closed circles
must be on
first part of
higher amount

Standard: Understand patterns, relations, and functions

Expectations: (a) Understand relations and functions and select and use various representations for them; (b) understand and compare the properties of classes of functions, including periodic functions

---

Standard: Analyze change in various contexts

Expectation: Approximate and interpret rates of change from graphical data

---

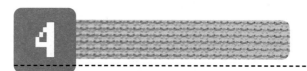

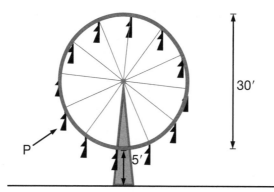

The Ferris wheel above is 30 feet in diameter and 5 feet above the ground. It turns at a steady rate of one revolution each 30 seconds. The graph that follows shows the distance from the ground of a person (P) as a function of time if the person is at the top of the Ferris wheel at time 0.

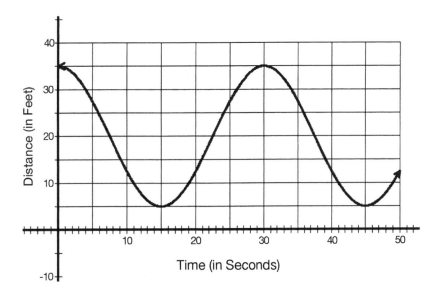

On the same graph draw a second curve that shows a person's distance from the ground as a function of time if that person is at the bottom of the Ferris wheel at time 0 and if the Ferris wheel turns at a steady rate of one revolution each 15 seconds.

Source: Adapted from *Results from the Seventh Mathematics Assessment of the National Assessment of Educational Progress* (Silver and Kenney 2000)
About the mathematics: This problem uses graph interpretation and allows us to assess whether students can understand and translate periodic graphs.
Solution

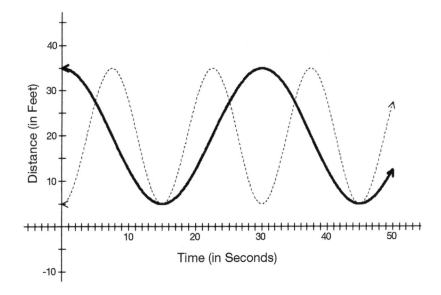

Student Work

Student A

This student gave a clear response and drew a fairly accurate graph.

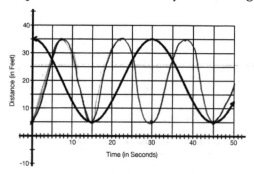

On the same graph draw a second curve that shows a person's distance from the ground, as a function of time, if that person is at the <u>bottom</u> of the Ferris wheel at time 0 and if the Ferris wheel turns at a steady rate of one revolution each _15_ seconds.

At the bottom of the ferris wheel the height is 5 feet and 15 sec. is twice as fast as 30 sec so there will be twice as many revolutions as before.

Student B

The explanation is correct, but the student started at $(0, 0)$ rather than $(0, 5)$. This error could be a reading mistake rather than a misconception in graph interpretation, but we do not know for sure. Having the student verbalize a slightly changed problem might help a teacher determine the source of the error.

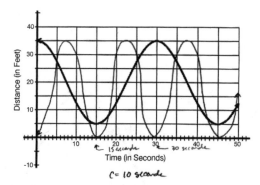

On the same graph draw a second curve that shows a person's distance from the ground, as a function of time, if that person is at the <u>bottom</u> of the Ferris wheel at time 0 and if the Ferris wheel turns at a steady rate of one revolution each _15_ seconds.

All I did was look at the original cosine curve and modeled the sine curve after it. I looked at the point where the cosine graph was completed, at 3c, and divided it by 2 (1.5c) to get 15 seconds of time. I then, starting at the origin, drew a sine graph that had a period of 1.5c, to model 1 revolution in 15 seconds.

Standard: Use mathematical models to represent and understand quantitative relationships

Expectations: (a) Identify essential quantitative relationships in a situation and determine a function that might model the relationship; (b) use symbolic expressions to represent relationships arising from various contexts; (c) draw reasonable conclusions about a situation being modeled

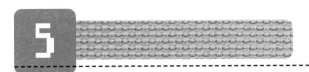

A cat ages faster than a human. To help us understand the age of our cats, cat years are sometimes compared with human years. Here are two models for comparing the age of cats with the age of humans.

Model 1: Each cat year is equivalent to 7 human years.

Model 2: The first year of a cat's life is the same as 15 human years. The second year of a cat's life is equivalent to 10 human years. Each additional cat year is equivalent to 4 human years.

a. Make a chart that compares cat years with human years for each model. Your chart should include at least four years.
b. Write an equation using each model for when the cat is 3 or more years old.
c. Which model has the cat aging faster after the first two years of the cat's life? Explain how you know.
d. Calculate the cat's age in human years if the cat is 10 years old, using both model 1 and model 2. Determine which model gives the greater age for the cat. Show all your work.
e. To the nearest month, how old will the cat be when both models give the cat the same human age? At what human age(s) does this outcome occur? Show your work.

Source: Adapted from *Big Sky STARS: Student and Teacher Assessment Resources* (Montana Council of Teachers of Mathematics 2003)

About the mathematics: This problem lends itself to both graphing and algebraic solutions. Although part e requires the use of algebra, other parts can be done by graphing. This item is also an excellent example of the use of slope. The problem uses dimensional analysis and demonstrates an appropriate use of a calculator. It also uses representations to model and interpret physical situations and allows students to organize and consolidate their mathematical thinking and then communicate their solutions. Chapter 6 contains a scoring rubric as well as several scored papers for this problem.

Solution

a. Make a chart that compares cat years with human years for each model. Your chart should include at least four years.

Year	1	2	3	4	5	6
Model 1	7	14	21	28	35	42
Model 2	15	25	29	33	37	41

b. Write an equation using each model for when the cat is 3 or more years old.

Model 1 *Model 2*
$c = 7h$ $c = 4h + 17$

c = cat's age, h = human years

c. Which model has the cat aging faster after the first two years of the cat's life? Explain how you know.

Model 1
Since slope is rate of change, model 1 has the cat aging faster, with a slope of 7.

Calculate the cat's age in human years if the cat is 10 years old, using both model 1 and model 2. Determine which model gives the greater age for the cat. Show all your work.

Model 1: $c = 7(10) = 70$ years
Model 2: $c = 4(10) + 17 = 40 + 17 = 57$ years

To the nearest month, how old will the cat be when both models give the cat the same human age? At what human age(s) does this outcome occur? Show your work.

$$7h = 4h + 17$$
$$3h = 17$$
$$h = {}^{17}/_3 = 5 \, {}^2/_3 = 5 \text{ years, 8 months}$$

$$c = {}^{17}/_3(7) = {}^{119}/_3 = 39 \, {}^2/_3$$
$$= 39 \text{ years, 8 months}$$

Student Work

Student A

The equations in part b do not fit the data in the charts in part a. The student did not answer the question that was asked in part c. In part d he was able to come up with the correct equation for model 1 but generated a second incorrect equation for model 2. His answer to part d is correct, but it was based on a faulty equation. In part e, he generated a third equation for one of the models. His answers are correct, but how he arrived at each new equation is difficult to understand. This student appears to need further instruction.

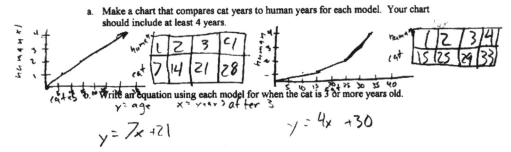

a. Make a chart that compares cat years to human years for each model. Your chart should include at least 4 years.

b. Write an equation using each model for when the cat is 3 or more years old.

$y = \text{age}$ $x = \text{years after 3}$

$$y = 7x + 21$$

$$y = 4x + 30$$

c. Which model has the cat aging faster after the first two years of the cat's life? Explain how you know.

2nd, graphs indicate/ after 2 years in the 1st, a cat is 14 yrs old in the 2nd model, the cat is 25 yrs old

d. Calculate the cat's age in human years if the cat is 10 years old using both Model 1 and Model 2. Determine which model gives the greatest age for the cat. Show all of your work.

Model 1 $y = 7x$ $10 = 7x$ $x = \frac{10}{7}$

Model 2 $y = 15x$ $10 = 15x$ $x = \frac{2}{3}$

$\boxed{\text{Model 1}}$

e. To the nearest month, how old will the cat be when both models give the cat the same human age? At what human age(s) does this occur? Show your work.

$y - 2 = \frac{1}{4}(x - 25)$ $y = \frac{1}{7}x$ $\frac{1}{7}x = \frac{1}{4}x - \frac{17}{4}$ $\frac{119}{3} = 7x$

$y - 2 = \frac{1}{4}x - \frac{23}{4}$ $-\frac{3}{28}x = \frac{57}{4}$ human years $= \frac{17}{3}$ yrs

$y = \frac{1}{4}x - \frac{17}{4}$ $x = \frac{119}{3}$ 5 yrs 8 months/August

cat 39 yrs 8 months/August

Student B

This student was unable to determine the equation for model 2, so she answered questions c–d by extending her chart, although her answer to part c is incorrect. Her response may indicate a need for further instruction on writing equations from data given in a table or interpreting data in table form.

a. **Make a chart that compares cat years to human years for each model. Your chart should include at least 4 years.**

Model 1

cat	1	2	3	4
human	7	14	21	28

cat	1	2	3	4
human	15	25	29	33

Model 2

b. **Write an equation using each model for when the cat is 3 or more years old.**

Model 1

$y = 7x$ $y =$

c. **Which model has the cat aging faster after the first two years of the cat's life? Explain how you know.**

Model 2, because the cat would be 25 human years old, and Model 1 says 14.

d. **Calculate the cat's age in human years if the cat is 10 years old using both Model 1 and Model 2. Determine which model gives the greatest age for the cat. Show all of your work.**

Model 1

$y = 7x$
$y = 7(10)$
$y = 70$ years old

cat	5	6	7	8	9	10
human	37	41	45	49	53	57

Model 2

$y = 57$ years old

e. **To the nearest month, how old will the cat be when both models give the cat the same human age? At what human age(s) does this occur? Show your work.**

cat	1	2	3	4	5	6	7	8	9	10
human	7	14	21	28	35	42	49	56	63	70

cat	1	2	3	4	5	6	7	8	9	10
human	15	25	29	33	37	41	45	49	53	57

Cat will be about 7 ½ years old, 49 human years
June

Standard: Represent and analyze mathematical situations and structures using algebraic symbols

Expectation: Use symbolic algebra to represent and explain mathematical relationships

Standard: Use mathematical models to represent and understand quantitative relationships

Expectations: (a) Identify essential quantitative relationships in a situation and determine a function that might model the relationship; (b) draw reasonable conclusions about a situation being modeled

6

Bill is on a hiking trip, where he hikes to the top of a large cliff (121 meters high) and accidentally drops his backpack off the edge. Sue is at the bottom of the cliff 43 meters from the base of the cliff. She sees what is happening and tries to catch the backpack. She runs toward the base of the cliff as fast as she can at the exact moment the backpack is dropped. After 1 second she is 35 meters away from the base.

a. Model Sue's distance from the base of the cliff as a linear function of the time she has been running. Identify what each variable in the function represents.

b. Use your model to predict how long Sue will take to reach the base of the cliff. Show your work.

c. After 1 second Bill's backpack is approximately 116 meters above the base of the cliff. After 2 seconds Bill's backpack is approximately 101 meters above the base of the cliff. Write a quadratic function that models the fall of Bill's backpack. Show your work, or explain your method.

d. Use your function from part c to predict how long Bill's backpack will take to reach the base of the cliff. Show your work.

e. Can Sue get to the base of the cliff in time to catch Bill's backpack? Justify your answer.

Source: *Adapted from Big Sky STARS: Student and Teacher Assessment Resources* (Montana Council of Teachers of Mathematics 2003)

Teacher note: An extension to this problem would be to ask students to calculate how fast the student at the bottom of the cliff is running and to determine whether this rate of speed is reasonable.

About the mathematics: The modeling aspect of this problem provides for different approaches: matrices, parametrics, or curve fitting. Students can solve the problem by graphing or by using a calculator to get regressions to find the functions. The problem could be extended by not specifying linear and quadratic functions in parts a and c, respectively. The problem also emphasizes the Process Standards of having students—

- use representations to model and interpret situations that arise in mathematics and in other contexts;

- monitor and reflect on the process of mathematical problem solving; and then

- communicate their mathematical thinking.

Chapter 6 contains a scoring rubric as well as several scored papers for this item.

Solution

a. Model Sue's distance from the base of the cliff as a linear function of the time she has been running. Identify what each variable in the function represents.

$$d = 43 - 8t$$

d is the distance in meters.

t is the time in seconds.

b. Use your model to predict how long Sue will take to reach the base of the cliff. Show your work.

$$43 - 8t = 0$$
$$43 = 8t$$
$${}^{43}/_8 = t$$
$$t = 5{}^3/_8$$

Sue will reach the base of the cliff in $5{}^3/_8$ seconds.

c. After 1 second Bill's backpack is approximately 116 meters above the base of the cliff. After 2 seconds Bill's backpack is approximately 101 meters above the base of the cliff. Write a quadratic function that models the fall of Bill's backpack. Show your work, or explain your method.

Vertex (0, 121) and passes through (1, 116)

$$y = a(t - 0)^2 + 121 \qquad \text{y is the distance above the ground.}$$
$$116 = a(1)^2 + 121 \qquad \text{t is the time in seconds.}$$
$$-5 = a$$
$$y = -5(t - 0)^2 + 121$$
$$y = -5t^2 + 121$$

d. Use your function from part c to predict how long Bill's backpack will take to reach the base of the cliff. Show your work.

$$-5t^2 + 121 = 0$$
$$121 = 5t^2$$
$$\frac{121}{5} = t^2$$
$$t = \sqrt{\frac{121}{5}} \approx 4.92 \text{ seconds}$$

Bill's backpack will take 4.92 seconds to reach the base of the cliff.

e. Can Sue get to the base of the cliff in time to catch Bill's backpack? Justify your answer.

No. Sue takes 5.375 seconds to reach the bottom of the cliff, but the backpack will reach the ground in 4.92 seconds.

Student Work

Student A

Student A gave complete answers and showed all work. The solution makes a nice use of matrices in part c.

a. Model Sue's distance from the base of the cliff as a linear function of the time she has been running. Identify what each variable in the function represents.

$(0, 43)$
$(1, 35)$

x: seconds after the backpack is dropped
y: meters away from the base

$y - 43 = \frac{35 - 43}{1 - 0}(x \cdot 0)$

Pt. Slope form

$$\boxed{y = -8x + 43}$$

b. Use your model to predict how long it will take Sue to reach the base of the cliff. Show your work.

$0 = -8x + 43$

$-43 = -8x$

$x = \frac{43}{8}$ $\boxed{x = 5.375 \text{ seconds}}$

c. After 1 second Bill's backpack is approximately 116 meters above the base of the cliff. After 2 seconds Bill's backpack is approximately 101 meters above the base of the cliff. Write a quadratic function that models the fall of Bill's backpack. Show your work or explain your method.

$(0, 121)$
$(1, 116)$
$(2, 101)$

x: seconds
y: meters

$$\boxed{y = -5x^2 + 121}$$

$y = Ax^2 + Bx + c$

$121 = c$

$116 = A + B + c$ Matrices $A = -5$ $B = 0$ $C = 121$

$101 = 4A + 2B + c$

$\begin{bmatrix} 0 & 0 & 1 & 121 \\ 1 & 1 & 1 & 116 \\ 4 & 2 & 1 & 101 \end{bmatrix}$ rref $\rightarrow \begin{bmatrix} 1 & 0 & 0 & -5 \\ 0 & 1 & 0 & 0 \\ 0 & 0 & 1 & 121 \end{bmatrix}$

d. Use your function from part c to predict how long it will take Bill's backpack to reach the base of the cliff. Show your work.

$0 = -5x^2 + 121$

$-121 = -5x^2$

$\frac{121}{5} = x^2$ $x = \frac{11}{\sqrt{5}}$ $x = 4.919 \text{ seconds}$

e. Can Sue get to the base of the cliff in time to catch Bill's backpack? Justify your answer.

It will take Sue 5.375 seconds to reach the base of the cliff and Bill's backpack will reach the base of the cliff in 4.919 seconds therefore, Sue cannot make it to the base of the cliff in time.

Student B

Student B appears to have subtracted incorrectly and got 10 m/sec instead of 8 m/sec. Parts a and b would have been correct had he used 8 instead of 10. On part c the student shows his understanding of quadratics, knowing that $y = -5x^2$ is the base equation and then translating the equation up 121, the height of the cliff. Part e might have been correct if not for the error in part a.

a. Model Sue's distance from the base of the cliff as a linear function of the time she has been running. Identify what each variable in the function represents.

Sue 10 m/s $D = 43 - 10x$

D - distance ~~Sue has traveled~~ from cliff
x - time in seconds
43 - distance to cliff
10x - distance Sue has traveled

b. Use your model to predict how long it will take Sue to reach the base of the cliff. Show your work.

$$0 = 43 - 10x$$
$$-43 = -10x$$
$$x = \frac{43}{10} \text{ seconds} = 4.3 \text{ seconds}$$

c. After 1 second Bill's backpack is approximately 116 meters above the base of the cliff. After 2 seconds Bill's backpack is approximately 101 meters above the base of the cliff. Write a quadratic function that models the fall of Bill's backpack. Show your work or explain your method.

in regular quadratic, chart goes (0,0)(1,1)(2,4)(3,9)...
the y value was multiplied by five in problem, thus the equation is multiplied by 5.

0,0   1,5   2,20

$$y = -5x^2 + 121$$

y = distance from ground
x = seconds from drop
121 = height of cliff
$-5x^2$ = distance backpack has traveled

d. Use your function from part c to predict how long it will take Bill's backpack to reach the base of the cliff. Show your work.

$$0 = -5x^2 + 121$$
$$-121 = -5x^2$$
$$24.2 = x^2$$
$$x = 4.92 \text{ seconds}$$

e. Can Sue get to the base of the cliff in time to catch Bill's backpack? Justify your answer.

yes, the time it takes Sue to get to the cliff is less than the time it takes the backpack to fall.

Student C

Student C was correct on the solutions to parts a and b, but the graph she made fit a line to the quadratic motion of the falling object. This graphing error may have led to the error in part c, where she wrote a linear equation even though the problem stated that the equation was quadratic. A conversation with the student would be helpful in understanding the errors made. The error in part c appears to have led to the remaining errors in the solution.

a. Model Sue's distance from the base of the cliff as a linear function of the time she has been running. Identify what each variable in the function represents.

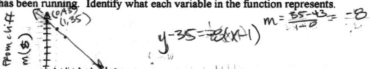

$$y - 35 = -8(x - 1) \qquad m = \frac{35 - 43}{1 - 0} = \frac{-8}{1} = -8$$

b. Use your model to predict how long it will take Sue to reach the base of the cliff. Show your work.

about 5 sec.

$$0 - 35 = -8(x - 1)$$
$$-35 = -\tfrac{1}{8}x + \tfrac{1}{8}$$
$$8x = 43$$
$$x = 5.375 \text{ sec}$$

c. After 1 second Bill's backpack is approximately 116 meters above the base of the cliff. After 2 seconds Bill's backpack is approximately 101 meters above the base of the cliff. Write a quadratic function that models the fall of Bill's backpack. Show your work or explain your method.

$$(2, 101)$$
$$(1, 116)$$
$$y - 101 = -15(x - 2)$$
$$m = \frac{116 - 101}{1 - 2}$$
$$= -15$$

d. Use your function from part c to predict how long it will take Bill's backpack to reach the base of the cliff. Show your work.

$$0 - 101 = -15(x - 2)$$
$$15x = 131$$
$$x = 8.733 \text{ sec.}$$

e. Can Sue get to the base of the cliff in time to catch Bill's backpack? Justify your answer.

Yes, she can reach the cliff in 5.4 sec, & Bill's backpack will reach it in 8.7 sec

Standard: Understand patterns, relations, and functions

Expectation: Generalize patterns using explicitly defined and recursively defined functions

Standard: Use mathematical models to represent and understand quantitative relationships

Expectations: (a) Identify essential quantitative relationships in a situation and determine a function that might model the relationship; (b) use symbolic expressions to represent relationships arising from various contexts; (c) draw reasonable conclusions about a situation being modeled

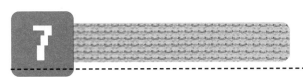

Upon taking his first job, Stuart Martin is given one of the following three options for his retirement plan.

Option A: $0.05 the first year
$0.15 the second year
$0.45 the third year
For every year following, triple the amount of the previous year.

Option B: $10 the first year
$20 the second year
$40 the third year
For every year following, double the amount of the previous year.

Option C: $100,000 the first year
$200,000 the second year
$300,000 the third year
For every year following, add $100,000 to the previous year's amount.

Your job is to give Stuart advice about which option is best. Using mathematics, show him which option is best for the short term and for the long term.

Source: Adapted from Oregon Department of Education
(www.ode.state.or.us/asmt/mathematics)

About the mathematics: Students must generate mathematical equations for each of the three different situations and then examine the long-term and short-term results to make decisions and answer the question. Teachers may want to give some guidance as to what might constitute "long term" and "short term." The solution to this problem bases the decision only on the amount the person receives each year but does not address the cumulative amount in the account. Students may want to explore this problem by looking at the cumulative amounts instead to see how this perspective might change their solution.

Solution

	Option A $y = \frac{1}{60} \cdot 3^x$	Option B $y = 5 \cdot 2^x$	Option C $y = 100{,}000 \cdot x$
Year 1	$ .05	$ 10	$100,000
Year 2	$ .15	$ 20	$200,000
Year 3	$ .45	$ 40	$300,000
Year 4	$1.35	$ 80	$400,000
Year 5	$4.05	$160	$500,000
$\vdots$	$\vdots$	$\vdots$	$\vdots$
Year 17	$2,152,336	$655,360	$1,700,000

Up to year 17, option C is best. But at year 17 and thereafter, option A is best. Option B is never a good choice.

Student Work

Student A

Student A used the correct formulas and justified his answers.

OPTION A   OPTION B   OPTION C

$y = \frac{1}{60} \cdot 3^x$ $y = 5 \cdot 2^x$ $y = 100,000 X$

THE BEST OPTION FOR THE SHORT TERM IS OPTION C. STUART WILL START OFF WITH A LARGE AMOUNT AND BY THE 10TH YEAR HE WILL RECIEVE 1 MILLION DOLLARS WHEREAS OPTION B AT 10 YEARS IS ONLY $5,120 AND OPTION A IS ONLY $984.15
IN THE LONG TERM OPTION A WILL BE THE BETTER OPTION, BY THE 17TH YEAR STUART WOULD RECIEVE 2.15 MILLION DOLLARS WHERE OPTION C HE'LL RECIEVE ONLY 1.7 MILLION DOLLARS

OPTION B IS OK, BUT STUART WON'T BE MAKING A MILLION UNTIL 18TH YEAR. AND OPTION A WILL HAVE TRIPLED FROM 2.15 MIL. TO 6.46 MIL.

Student B

The student worked the problem without writing down any formulas and then summed the amounts. Whether her answer was based on the summed totals or on the amount determined by the year is unclear. The student neglected to justify her answer.

A	B	C	
		100 k	short term
.05	10	200 K	
.15	20	300 k	Plan C
.45	40	300 k	
.45	70. —	600 K	Long term
.65		400 K	Plan A
4th 1.75	80	500 K	
5th 4.05	160	600 K	
6th 12.15	320	700 K	
7th 36.45	640	800 K	
8th 109.35	1280	900 K	
9th 328.05	2560	1000 K	
10th 984.15	5120	1100 K	
11th 2925.45	10240	1200 K	
12th 8857.35	20480	1300 K	
13th 26572.05	40960	1400 K	
14th 79,716.15	81920		
15th 239148.45	163840	1500 K	
16th 717 445.35	327680	1600 K	
17th 2152336.05	655360	1700 k	
18th 6457008.15	1310720	1800 K	
19th 19371624.45	2621440	1900 k	
20th 58113873.35	5252880	2000 K	

8 7,169,583   10,495,750   21,000,000

Student C

The equations are correct, but the answer is not completely correct. The student did not explain his answer, "20 years." His reason why B is not a good choice is faulty. The explanation about option C appears to show an understanding of exponential growth.

Option A

$y = 3^{x-1} \times .05$

is the best option for long term (more than 20 years)
However you start very small but by the 20th
year the annual income is larger than the two other options.
It will grow rapidly and make up for the
small income during the first 20 years.

Option B

$y = 2^{x-1} \times 10$ is not a good choice. It surpasses
Option A in the 19th year but is soon behind option A

Option C is the best for short term
$y = 100,000x$. Because it is not exponential
it will not increase as quickly as the others
over a long period of time. However, it is
the best for 20 years or less because you
begin with the most money.

Standard: Represent and analyze mathematical situations and structures using algebraic symbols

Expectation: Use symbolic algebra to represent and explain mathematical relationships

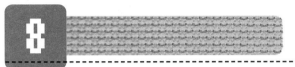

When trying to weigh some goods, a shopkeeper found that his balance scale was slightly bent, with one arm of the scale longer than the other. He was not worried until a customer ordered two pounds of nuts, which unfortunately were not packaged. The shopkeeper stated that he would take a one-pound weight and put it on the right side of the scale and balance it on the left with nuts. He then stated he would put the same one-pound weight on the left side of the scale and balance it on the right with nuts. He told the customer that he was sure that together the two packages would weigh more than two pounds.

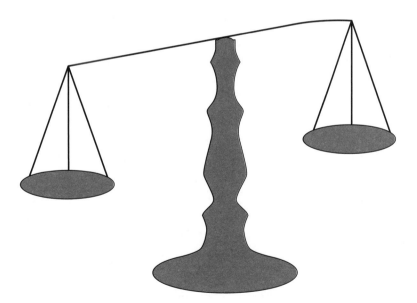

Would you advise the customer to accept the deal? Explain using mathematical language how you reached your conclusion.

Source: Adapted from *Balanced Assessment for the Twenty-first Century* (Schwartz and Kenney 2000, p. 166, problem HL069). These tasks were developed with the support of the National Science Foundation. Copyright © 1995–2000 by President and Fellows of Maryland College. All rights reserved. Used with permission.

About the mathematics: This good nonstandard problem has multiple solution methods and makes many connections with other topics. It also allows students to demonstrate their ability to analyze a situation and choose the appropriate mathematics needed to answer the question posed.

Solution: The customer should accept the deal.

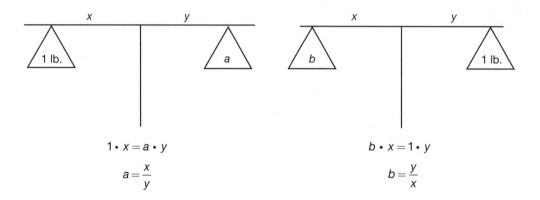

$$1 \cdot x = a \cdot y$$

$$a = \frac{x}{y}$$

$$b \cdot x = 1 \cdot y$$

$$b = \frac{y}{x}$$

To be fair, $a + b$ must be greater than or equal to 2. Since

$$b = \frac{1}{a},$$

we have

$$a + \frac{1}{a} \geq 2,$$

$$a^2 + 1 \geq 2a,$$

$$a^2 - 2a + 1 \geq 0,$$

$$(a - 1)^2 \geq 0.$$

Since this result is always true, the customer should take the deal.

Standard: Understand patterns, relations, and functions

Expectation: Generalize patterns using explicitly defined and recursively defined functions

Standard: Use mathematical models to represent and understand quantitative relationships

Expectations: (a) Identify essential quantitative relationships in a situation and determine a function that might model the relationship; (b) use symbolic expressions to represent relationships arising from various contexts; (c) draw reasonable conclusions about a situation being modeled

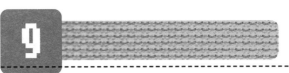

On the first day of school Lise's teacher asks the students what $1 + 1$ equals, and the students reply 2. The next day the teacher asks what $2 + 2$ equals, and the students reply 4. The next day the teacher asks what $4 + 3$ equals, and the students reply 7. The teacher continues this questioning on each day of school by taking the sum from the previous day and adding the day of school to yield the following pattern:

Sum from Previous Day		Day in the School Year		Sum
1	+	1	=	2
2	+	2	=	4
4	+	3	=	7
7	+	4	=	11
11	+	5	=	16

If the school year has 180 days, what will be the sum on the last day of school?

About the mathematics: Once students determine the pattern, they can solve the problem in multiple ways: elimination, matrices, or calculators using regression. The problem helps students understand how mathematical ideas interconnect and build on one another to produce an answer.

Solution

To arrive at an algebraic expression that will give us the 180th term of the sequence, we examine the sums to ascertain whether they are either arithmetic or geometric. Since they are neither, we try a difference table.

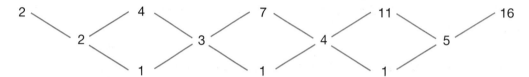

Because we arrive at a constant in the second row of the difference table, we know that the algebraic expression we are looking for is quadratic. We can find this expression by using the first three points, (1, 2), (2, 4), and (3, 7). Placing these values in the general form $ax^2 + bx + c = y$, we arrive at the three equations

$$1a + 1b + c = 2,$$
$$4a + 2b + c = 4,$$

and

$$9a + 3b + c = 7$$

and can solve for our expression by using elimination or matrices. We can also put 1, 2, and 3 in List 1 on our calculator, put 2, 4, and 7 in List 2 on our calculator, and do a quadratic regression. Either way, the algebraic expression is

$$\frac{1}{2}x^2 + \frac{1}{2}x + 1.$$

Therefore, the sum for the 180th day of school is 16,291.

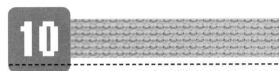

Standard: Understand patterns, relations, and numbers

Expectation: Generalize patterns using explicitly defined and recursively defined functions

10

Given the following pinball arrangement, how many different paths can a ball travel from the top to the bottom? A move can be made only to a spot diagonally adjacent and below. We start at row 0 because our first move takes us to the next row.

If this pattern continues to row 15, how many different paths will result? Write a general rule for calculating the number of possible paths, p, in relation to the number of rows, r.

About the mathematics: The student can trace the paths to generate a table from which to generalize to the algebraic form of the solution. The problem can also be related to Pascal's triangle, since the number of paths corresponds to the sum of the elements in each row of the triangle.

Solution: We first set up a set of ordered pairs to reflect the number of paths for the first several rows (r, p), assuming that the top is row 0: (0, 1), (1, 2), (2, 4), (3, 8), (4, 16). From the ordered pairs, we see that the general rule for possible paths (p) in relation to the number of rows (r) is $p = 2^r$. For row 15, we would obtain 2^{15}, or 32,768, different paths.

Standard: Represent and analyze mathematical situations and structures using algebraic symbols

Expectation: Use symbolic algebra to represent and explain mathematical relationships

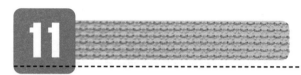

For each of the following, sketch the graph of a function—
a. that always increases and is never negative;
b. whose graph lies in exactly two quadrants;
c. that is quadratic and whose graph lies in exactly three quadrants;
d. having both positive and negative values that are never greater than 1 or smaller than –1;
e. that looks exactly the same when shifted to the right (by any amount);
f. that is quadratic and never intersects the *x*-axis;
g. that looks the same when reflected in a mirror that lies along the *y*-axis.

Source: Adapted from *Balanced Assessment for the Twenty-first Century* (Schwartz and Kenney 2000, p. 129, problem HC011). These tasks were developed with the support of the National Science Foundation. Copyright © 1995–2000 by President and Fellows of Maryland College. All rights reserved. Used with permission.

About the mathematics: This problem assesses students' understanding of the graphs of functions. The problem is easily extended, for example, "Sketch the graph of a function that has no real roots." Because answers can vary, the problem allows students to share answers and determine what is the same and different about the graphs. The problem is also good for classroom discussions about the characteristics of functions and their graphs. Calculators can be used for trial and error as students search for functions satisfying the different conditions.

Solution: Answers vary.

Standard: Represent and analyze mathematical situations and structures using algebraic symbols

Expectation: Use symbolic algebra to represent and explain mathematical relationships

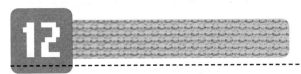

For each of the following, write a symbolic expression (i.e., a formula) for a function—

a. that always increases and is never negative;
b. whose graph lies in exactly two adjacent quadrants;
c. whose graph lies in exactly two nonadjacent quadrants;
d. whose graph lies in exactly three quadrants;
e. that is quadratic and whose graph lies in exactly two quadrants;
f. that is quadratic and whose graph lies in exactly three quadrants;
g. that is quadratic and whose graph lies in all four quadrants;
h. that has a graph that looks like the letter V.

Source: Adapted from *Balanced Assessment for the Twenty-first Century* (Schwartz and Kenney 2000, p. 129, problem HC011). These tasks were developed with the support of the National Science Foundation. Copyright © 1995–2000 by President and Fellows of Maryland College. All rights reserved. Used with permission.

About the mathematics: This item could be used with the previous problem to have students go back and forth between graphs of functions and their symbolic expressions. The item could be extended by asking students for more generalized solutions.

Possible solutions

a. $y = 2^x$
b. $x = 1$
c. $y = x$
d. $y = x^3 + 1$
e. $y = (x - 1)^2$
f. $y = (x - 1)^2 - 1$
g. $y = x^2 - 2$
h. $y = |x|$

> **Standard:** Represent and analyze mathematical situations and structures using algebraic symbols

> **Expectations:** (a) Use symbolic algebra to represent and explain mathematical relationships; (b) judge the meaning, utility, and reasonableness of the results of symbol manipulation, including those carried out by technology

> **Standard:** Use mathematical models to represent and understand quantitative relationships

> **Expectations:** (a) Use symbolic expressions to represent relationships from various contexts; (b) draw reasonable conclusions about a situation being modeled

13

If a certain medicine is absorbed by your body at a rate so that $1/3$ of the original amount is left after 8 hours and if your doctor gives you 10 grams today and does not want more than 10 grams to accumulate in your system, how much medicine should she give you tomorrow at the same time?

About the mathematics: Although the problem could be worked as an exponential function, it is accessible to beginning algebra students.

Solution

After 8 hours:

$$\frac{1}{3}(10) \approx 3.3 \text{ grams left}$$

After 16 hours:

$$\frac{1}{3}\left(\frac{1}{3}(10)\right) \approx 1.1 \text{ grams left}$$

After 24 hours:

$$\frac{1}{3}\left(\frac{1}{3}\left(\frac{1}{3}(10)\right)\right) \approx 0.37 \text{ grams left}$$

10 grams − 0.37 = 9.73 grams

Standard: Understand patterns, relations, and numbers

Expectations: (a) Generalize patterns using explicitly defined and recursively defined functions; (b) analyze functions of one variable by investigating rates of change

Standard: Represent and analyze mathematical situations and structures using algebraic symbols

Expectation: Use symbolic algebra to represent and explain mathematical relationships

Standard: Use mathematical models to represent and understand quantitative relationships

Expectation: Use symbolic expressions to represent relationships from various contexts

Standard: Analyze change in various contexts

Expectation: Approximate and interpret rates of change from graphical and numerical data

(Continued on page 60)

(Continued from page 59)

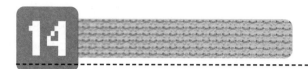

A gardener plants tomatoes in a square pattern. To protect the tomatoes from insects, she surrounds the tomatoes with marigolds. The diagram below shows the pattern of tomato plants and marigolds for any number (*n*) of rows of tomato plants. Find the number of marigolds on the basis of the number of tomato plants.

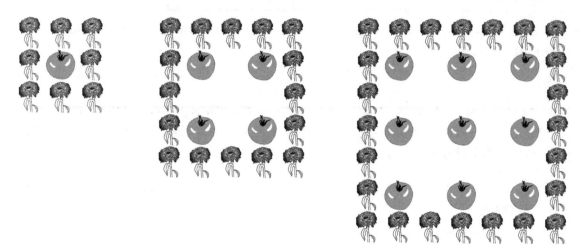

About the mathematics: This problem is so rich that it overlaps several Standards and Expectations. To answer the question, students need to make a table to see the pattern and then generate the function that describes the pattern.

Solution

We first order the pairs (t, m): (1, 8), (4, 16), (9, 24). The regression feature of the calculator can be used to find the square-root function that best models these ordered pairs:

$$m = 8\sqrt{t}$$

Standard: Understand patterns, relations, and functions

Expectations: (a) Generalize patterns using explicitly defined and recursively defined functions; (b) analyze functions of one variable by investigating rates of change

Standard: Represent and analyze mathematical situations and structures using algebraic symbols

Expectation: Use symbolic algebra to represent and understand mathematical relationships

Standard: Use mathematical models to represent and understand quantitative relationships

Expectation: Use symbolic expressions to represent relationships from various contexts

Standard: Analyze change in various contexts

Expectation: Approximate and interpret rates of change from graphical and numerical data

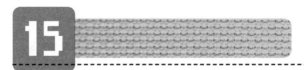

15

The population of the world was 3.9 billion in 1970 and 6.3 billion in 2000. If the rate of growth is assumed proportional to the number present, what estimate would you give for the population in 2020? Some researchers estimate that the earth can sustain a maximum population of 50 billion. If the population growth continues at the same rate, when will the earth's population reach 50 billion?

About the mathematics: This problem allows students to see the importance of the exponential growth model and the practical uses of the natural logarithm in solving such problems. An extension of the problem would be to discuss the logistic growth models and why they capture the essence of growth problems better than the standard exponential models.

Solution

We know that the formula for exponential growth is

$$P = P_0 e^{kt},$$

$$6.3 = 3.9 e^{k(30)},$$

$$\frac{6.3}{3.9} = e^{30k};$$

or

$$\ln\frac{6.3}{3.9} = 30k;$$

or

$$k \approx 0.016.$$

Estimate for 2020:

$$P = 3.9 e^{(.016)(50)},$$

or approximately 8.7 billion. If growth continues at this same rate, the population will reach 50 billion in—

$$50 = 3.9 e^{(.016)t},$$

$$\frac{50}{3.9} = e^{.016t},$$

$$\ln\frac{50}{3.9} = 0.016t,$$

or $t \approx 159$ years. Adding gives 1970 + 159, or the year 2129.

(If students know how to solve differential equations, they can derive the formula from the statement "the rate of growth is assumed proportional to the number present," or $dP/dt = kP$.)

Standard: Use mathematical models to represent and understand quantitative relationships

Expectations: (a) Identify essential quantitative relationships in a situation and determine the class or classes of functions that might model the relationship; (b) draw reasonable conclusions about a situation being modeled

16

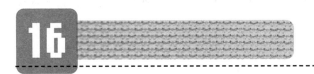

Bill's house is 5 miles east-northeast of town, and Sue's house is due east of town on Highway 63. A straight dirt road from Bill's house to Sue's house is 7 miles long. What angle does the dirt road make with Highway 63?

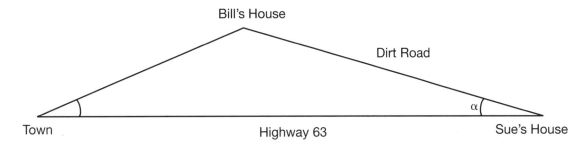

About the mathematics: The complexity of the problem can increase by changing the distance from Bill's house to Sue's house to 2 miles. This modification makes the problem an ambiguous case with two possible solutions. To lower the level of complexity, students might need to be given that east-northeast represents an angle of 22.5 degrees.

Solution: Students must understand that east-northeast of town indicates an angle of 22.5 degrees. The law of sines can then be used to solve the problem.

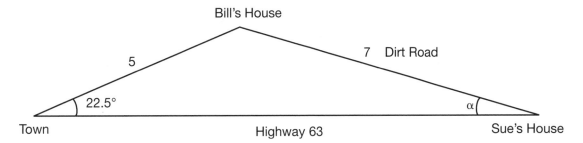

$$\frac{\sin(22.5°)}{7} = \frac{\sin\alpha}{5}$$

$$5(\sin(22.5°)) = 7\sin\alpha$$

$$\sin\alpha = 5 \cdot \frac{\sin(22.5°)}{7} \approx 0.273$$

Using inverse sine, we get

$$\alpha = 15.86°.$$

Standard: Understand patterns, relations, and functions

Expectation: Analyze functions of one variable by investigating rates of change

---

Standard: Represent and analyze mathematical situations and structures using algebraic symbols

Expectations: (a) Use symbolic algebra to represent and explain mathematical relationships; (b) judge the meaning, utility, and reasonableness of the results of symbol manipulatives, including those carried out by technology

---

Designs for the locations of communications towers, aerial tramways, ski lifts, and air lanes all depend on establishing the equation of a line of sight. Suppose that a section of the Rocky Mountains has the skyline described by the graph of

$$y = -x^4 - 2x^3 + 12x^2 + x - 10$$

for $-4 < x < 3$. Find an equation that represents the line of sight that just grazes the two mountain peaks.

About the mathematics: Because the solution does not use the maximum values of the graph, it is best solved by successive approximations of equations of lines that touch both peaks in the range. Students can guess an equation of a line and then use their calculators to successively refine that guess to find an equation that works.

Solution: With a graphing calculator, students can use trial and error with lines to see which one will match up best as a line of sight. One answer is

$$y = -12.09x + 30.8.$$

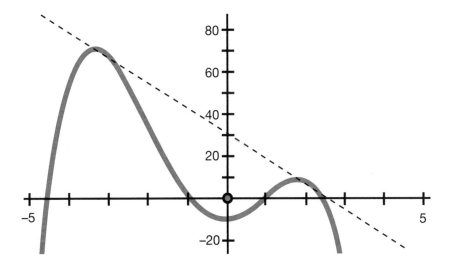

Standard: Use mathematical models to represent and understand quantitative relationships

Expectations: (a) Identify essential quantitative relationships in a situation and determine the class or classes of functions that might model the relationship; (b) use symbolic expressions to represent relationships arising from various contexts; (c) draw reasonable conclusions about a situation being modeled

18

When an earthquake occurs, energy waves radiate in concentric circles from the epicenter, the point above where the earthquake occurred. Stations with seismographs record the level of that energy and the length of time the energy took to reach the station.

a. Suppose that one station determines that the epicenter of an earthquake is about 200 miles from the station. Find an equation for the possible location of the epicenter.
b. A second station, 120 miles east and 160 miles north of the first station, shows the epicenter to be about 235 miles away. Find an equation for the possible location of the epicenter.
c. Using the information from parts a and b, find the possible locations of the epicenter.

> **Source:** Adapted from *Enhancing Teacher Quality: Algebra II* (Charles A. Dana Center 2004, task 7.4.2). This item was developed with support (in part) from the Texas Higher Education Coordinating Board. Used with permission.
>
> **About the mathematics:** This problem uses conic sections (circles), their geometric properties, and algebraic representations to model physical situations and solve application problems. Students must first realize that circles will model the problem, next should write the equations, and then should solve the problem either algebraically or graphically. They may need to be reminded that the solutions must then be interpreted in light of the problem to answer the questions. Teachers may need to give the hint that the first station should be placed at the origin.

Solution

a. The epicenter lies on the circle $x^2 + y^2 = 200^2$.

b. The epicenter lies on the circle $(x - 120)^2 + (y - 160)^2 = 235^2$.

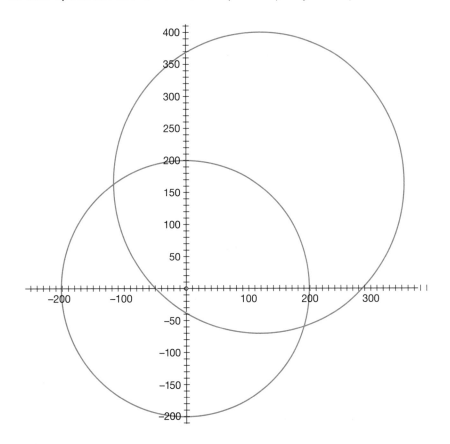

c. The approximate solutions to the systems are (–114.97, 163.65) and (189.30, –64.55). If we put these answers into the context of the problem, we have two possibilities for the epicenter: approximately 114.97 miles west and 163.65 miles north of the first station or approximately 189.30 miles east and 64.55 miles south of the first station.

Geometry

THE SAMPLER problems in this chapter focus on the Geometry Standards from *Principles and Standards for School Mathematics* (NCTM 2000) and are intended to assist classroom teachers as they develop expertise in implementing standards-based assessment for geometry. Students must analyze and use properties and relationships of two- and three-dimensional geometric shapes; understand transformations through sketches, coordinates, vectors, and matrices; use constructions to explore geometric relationships; and solve problems using modeling and mathematical reasoning. The problems also require that students formulate and explore conjectures about geometric shapes and figures as they learn that geometry provides a means of describing, analyzing, and understanding their surroundings. Since communicating convincing mathematical arguments is central to the study of geometry, students are required to produce logical arguments and present them effectively with careful explanations of their reasoning, with either paragraph or two-column proofs.

Three of the thirteen problems are in multiple-choice format and require justifications and multiple-step solutions. Justifications are to be written clearly and precisely, using correct mathematical vocabulary and proper notation. A problem requiring formal proof is also included in this sampler to emphasize the importance of proofs, deductive reasoning, and more formal reasoning techniques to solve problems. Two problems are of the short-response type, and eight are of the extended–response type. Four of the thirteen items are cross-listed in chapter 4, "Measurement." A "challenger" problem involving geometric probability is cross-listed with chapter 5, "Data Analysis and Probability."

Geometry Assessment Items

Standard: Analyze characteristics and properties of two- and three-dimensional geometric shapes and develop mathematical arguments about geometric relationships

Expectations: (a) Analyze properties and determine attributes of two- and three-dimensional objects, (b) explore relationships (including congruence and similarity) of two-and three-dimensional objects and solve problems involving them

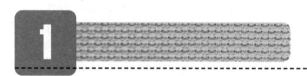

$\overline{AB}$ is the diameter of a semicircle k, C is an arbitrary point on the semicircle (other than A or B), and S is the center of the circle inscribed in triangle ABC.

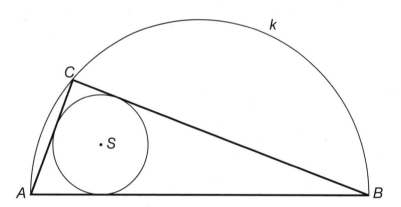

Which of the following must be true?
a. The measure of angle ASB changes as C moves on k.
b. The measure of angle ASB is the same for all positions of C, but it cannot be determined without knowing the radius.
c. The measure of angle ASB is 135° for all C.
d. The measure of angle ASB is 150° for all C.

Justify your answer.

Source: Adapted from TIMSS Population 3 Item Pool (K-10)

About the mathematics: This problem presents an opportunity for students to use dynamic software. It employs students' knowledge of geometry, specifically their understanding of triangles inscribed in a semicircle and circles inscribed in a triangle, properties of tangency, and relationships between geometric figures. It also allows students to apply and adapt a variety of appropriate strategies to solve problems, select and use various types of reasoning and methods of proof, and communicate their mathematical thinking to others.

Solution: c

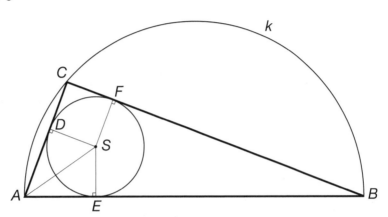

Triangles *SAD* and *SAE* are congruent by SAS because the radii are congruent and segments *AE* and *AD* are congruent. (Tangents drawn to a circle from a point outside the circle are congruent.) Therefore $\angle A$ is bisected. The same reasoning could be used to show that triangles *SBE* and *SBF* (not shown) are congruent, so that $\angle B$ is bisected.

$$m\angle ASB = 180 - \left(\frac{1}{2}m\angle A + \frac{1}{2}m\angle B\right),$$

$$m\angle ASB = 180 - \frac{1}{2}(m\angle A + m\angle B).$$

But

$$m\angle A + m\angle B = 90,$$

$$m\angle ASB = 180 - \frac{1}{2}(90),$$

$$m\angle ASB = 180 - 45 = 135.$$

Student Work

Student A

This student needs to explain why the segments *SA* and *SB* bisect angles *A* and *B*, respectively.

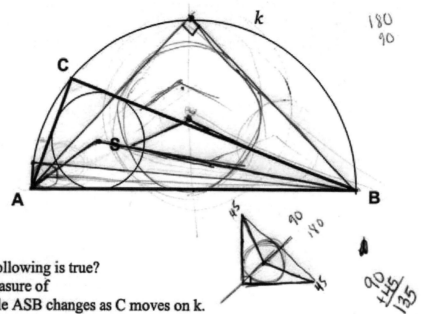

Which of the following is true?
The measure of
    a. angle ASB changes as C moves on k.
    b. angle ASB is the same for all positions of C but it cannot be determined without knowing the radius.
    c. the measure of angle ASB is 135° for all C.
    d. the measure of angle ASB is 150° for all C.
Justify your answer.

the 90° triangle from the circle has 180° in it so subtracting ½ of the 2 other angles then adding that to the 90° gives you 135°. therefore ASB is the same for all positions and has a measure of angle of 135°.

Student B

The responses of students B and C reflect the incorrect reasoning that is probably typical of most geometry students. Student B was able to see that angle *ASB* would remain the same but did not see the relationship between the center of the inscribed circle and the segments to the vertices of angles *A* and *B*.

As arbitrary point C moves on semi-circle k, angle ACB remains the same 90° because its intercepted arc is a semi-circle. However, ∠'s CAB and ABC change, but still remain complementary to angle ACB. As point C moves, point S remains stationary and so do points A and B—because of this angle ASB remains the same. There is no way to figure out the measure of angle ASB with the given information, but with the knowledge of the radius' measure angle ASB can be determined.

Student C

Student C's reasoning was also incorrect. The student understood that angles *A* and *B* change as *C* moves but did not realize that angle *ASB* would not, because it does not stay in the same line.

As C moves the Angles A + B will either increase or decrease making the circle s larger or smaller, which in return will increase or decrease the radius of of s and change the measure of angle ASB.

Standard: Analyze characteristics and properties of two- and three-dimensional geometric shapes and develop mathematical arguments about geometric relationships

Expectation: Analyze properties and determine attributes of two- and three-dimensional objects

Standard: Specify locations and describe spatial relationships using coordinate geometry and other representational systems

Expectation: Use Cartesian coordinates and other coordinate systems to analyze geometric situations

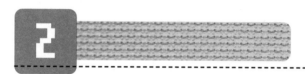

The vertices of the triangle PQR are the points $P(1, 2)$, $Q(4, 6)$, and $R(-4, 12)$. Which one of the following statements about triangle PQR must be true?

a. PQR is a right triangle with the right angle at P.
b. PQR is a right triangle with the right angle at Q.
c. PQR is a right triangle with the right angle at R.
d. PQR is not a right triangle.

Justify your answer.

> **Source:** TIMSS Population 3 Item Pool (K-7)
> **About the mathematics:** This problem has multiple solution methods. It also involves a good application of the Pythagorean theorem and allows students to demonstrate their understanding of right angles and right triangles and of their properties.
>
> **Solution:** b

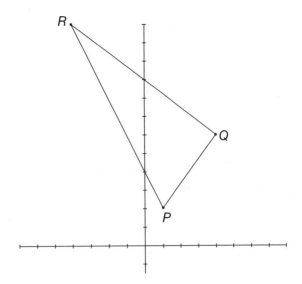

Since $\overline{PQ} \perp \overline{QR}$, $\triangle PQR$ is a right triangle with the right angle at Q.

Student Work

Student A

This student used the approach of finding slopes of the lines to choose his answer (although he made an arithmetic error on the slope of $\overline{PR}$).

    a. PQR is a right triangle with the right angle at P.
    (b.) PQR is a right triangle with the right angle at Q.
    c. PQR is a right triangle with the right angle at R.
    d. PQR is not a right triangle.

Justify your answer.

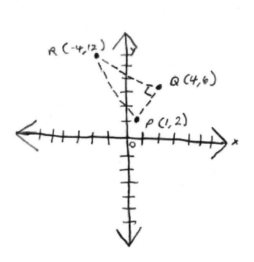

$$m\,PR = \frac{y_2 - y_1}{x_2 - x_1} = \frac{2-12}{1+4} = \frac{-14}{6}$$

$$m\,QP = \frac{y_2 - y_1}{x_2 - x_1} = \frac{6-2}{4-1} = \frac{4}{3}$$

$$m\,RQ = \frac{y_2 - y_1}{x_2 - x_1} = \frac{12-6}{4-4} = \frac{6}{-8} = -\frac{3}{4}$$

$\overline{QP} \perp \overline{RQ}$, which makes a $90°$ angle.

Student B

This work is great—but the student marked the wrong answer, probably as the result of a careless mistake. The teacher would not know the student's level of understanding without seeing her work. This example underscores the importance of having students justify their answers, even for multiple-choice questions.

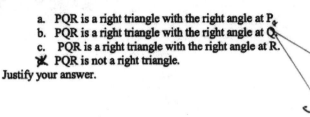

a. PQR is a right triangle with the right angle at P.
b. PQR is a right triangle with the right angle at Q.
c. PQR is a right triangle with the right angle at R.
✗ PQR is not a right triangle.

Justify your answer.

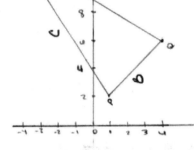

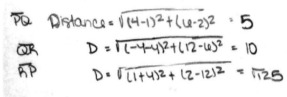

$\overline{PQ}$ Distance $= \sqrt{(4-1)^2 + (6-2)^2} = 5$

$\overline{QR}$ $D = \sqrt{(-4-4)^2 + (12-6)^2} = 10$

$\overline{RP}$ $D = \sqrt{(1+4)^2 + (2-12)^2} = \sqrt{125}$

The answer is B.

slope $\dfrac{y_2 - y_1}{x_2 - x_1}$

$\overline{PQ}$: $\dfrac{6-2}{4-1} = \dfrac{4}{3}$

$\overline{RQ} = \dfrac{12-6}{-4-4} = -\dfrac{6}{8} = -\dfrac{3}{4}$

Since the slope of the lines $\overline{PQ}$ & $\overline{RQ}$ are negative reciprocals, they are perpendicular and make a right angle at point Q. Also, if you use the $A^2 + B^2 = C^2$ formula, you get the correct length for side C.

$5^2 + 10^2 = C^2$

$25 + 100 = C^2$

$\sqrt{125} = C^2$

$C = \sqrt{125}$

Student C

An important point to emphasize to students is that answers should not be based on drawings.

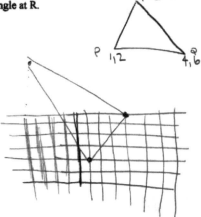

a. PQR is a right triangle with the right angle at P.
b. PQR is a right triangle with the right angle at Q.
c. PQR is a right triangle with the right angle at R.
d. PQR is not a right triangle.
Justify your answer.

none of them line up correctly

Standard: Specify locations and describe spatial relationships using coordinate geometry and other representational systems

Expectations: (a) Use Cartesian coordinates and other coordinate systems to analyze geometric situations; (b) solve problems using two- and three-dimensional objects represented in Cartesian coordinates

---

3

The rectangular coordinates of three points in a plane are $Q(-3, -1)$, $R(-2, 3)$, and $S(1, -3)$. A fourth point T is chosen so that vector ST is equal to twice vector QR. The y-coordinate of T is _____.

a. −11
b. −7
c. −1
d. 1
e. 5

Show how you got your answer.

Source: TIMSS Population 3 Item Pool (L-8)

About the mathematics: This item emphasizes and supports vectors in the curriculum and allows students to demonstrate their understanding of vectors, their properties, and vector equations.

Solution: e

$$\overrightarrow{QR} = (-2 + {}^{+}3, 3 + {}^{+}1) = (1, 4)$$
$$\overrightarrow{ST} = 2\,(1, 4) = (2, 8)$$
$(2, 8) = (x - 1, y - {}^{-}3)$
$x - 1 = 2 \qquad y + 3 = 8$
$\qquad x = 3 \qquad\qquad y = 5$
So T is $(3, 5)$.

Student Work

The correct solutions of students A, B, and C typify the different ways to solve the problem.

Student A

a. –11
b. –7
c. –1
d. 1
e. 5

$$\text{distance} = \sqrt{(x_2 - x_1)^2 + (y^2 - y_1)^2}$$

$$d = \sqrt{(-3 + 2)^2 + (-1 - 3)^2}$$

$$d = \sqrt{1 + 16}$$

$$d = \sqrt{17}$$

$$d \approx 4.123 \text{ of } QR$$

Original (y):
$= (-1 - 3)^2$
$= {}^{+}4^2$
$= 16$

New (y):
$= (-3 - 5)^2$
$= -8$
$= 64$

vector of $ST \approx 8.246$

$$d = \sqrt{(1 - ?)^2 + (-3 - ?)^2}$$

$$d = \sqrt{(1 - 0)^2 + (-3 - 5)^2}$$

$$d = \sqrt{1 + 64}$$

$$d \approx 8.062 \text{ of } ST$$

Student B

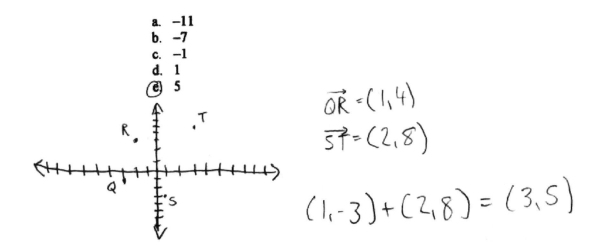

a. −11
b. −7
c. −1
d. 1
ⓔ 5

$$\vec{QR} = (1,4)$$
$$\vec{ST} = (2,8)$$

$$(1,-3) + (2,8) = (3,5)$$

Student C

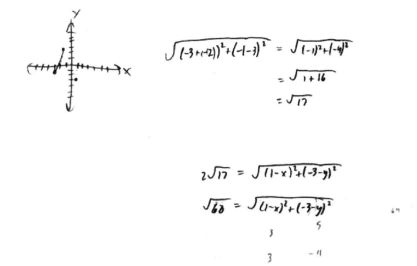

$$\sqrt{(-3+(-2))^2 + (-1-3)^2} = \sqrt{(-1)^2 + (-4)^2}$$
$$= \sqrt{1+16}$$
$$= \sqrt{17}$$

$$2\sqrt{17} = \sqrt{(1-x)^2 + (-3-y)^2}$$
$$\sqrt{68} = \sqrt{(1-x)^2 + (-3-y)^2}$$

3   5
3   −11

The y-coordinate being 5 makes double the move as vector QR (QR is right 1 up 4 + ST has to be right 2 up 8). It fits the requirements to get $2\sqrt{17}$ or $\sqrt{68}$ with 3 as the x-coordinate.

Student D

Student D showed some definite understanding of vectors but did not find the correct solution. His method uses a somewhat "guess and check" type of approach.

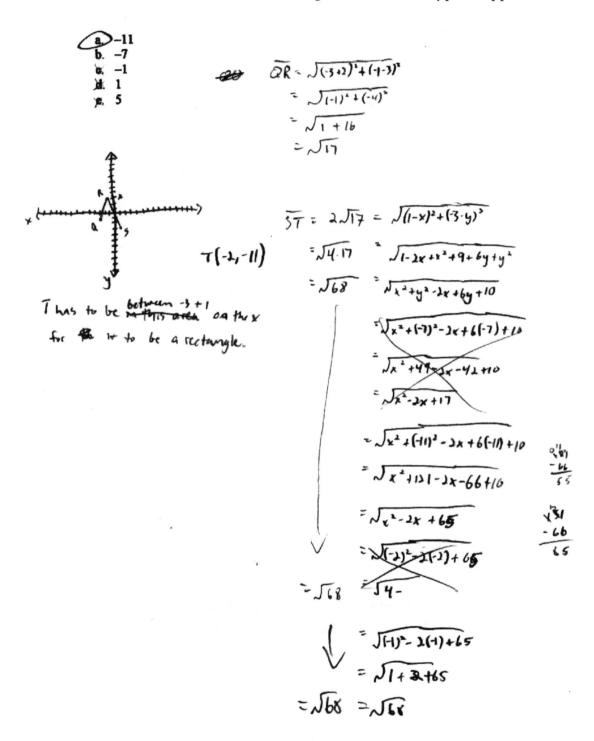

a. -11
b. -7
c. -1
d. 1
e. 5

$\overline{QR} = \sqrt{(-3+2)^2 + (-1-3)^2}$
$= \sqrt{(-1)^2 + (-4)^2}$
$= \sqrt{1 + 16}$
$= \sqrt{17}$

$T(-2, -11)$

This has to be between -3 $+1$ on the x for it to be a rectangle.

$\overline{ST} = 2\sqrt{17} = \sqrt{(1-x)^2 + (3-y)^2}$
$= \sqrt{4 \cdot 17} \quad = \sqrt{1 - 2x + x^2 + 9 + 6y + y^2}$
$= \sqrt{68} \quad = \sqrt{x^2 + y^2 - 2x + 6y + 10}$

$= \sqrt{x^2 + (-7)^2 - 2x + 6(-7) + 10}$
$= \sqrt{x^2 + 49 - 2x - 42 + 10}$
$= \sqrt{x^2 - 2x + 17}$

$= \sqrt{x^2 + (-11)^2 - 2x + 6(-11) + 10}$
$= \sqrt{x^2 + 121 - 2x - 66 + 10}$
$= \sqrt{x^2 - 2x + 65}$
$= \sqrt{(-2)^2 - 2(-2) + 65}$
$= \sqrt{68} \quad \sqrt{4 -}$

$= \sqrt{(-1)^2 - 2(-1) + 65}$
$= \sqrt{1 + 2 + 65}$
$= \sqrt{68} \quad = \sqrt{68}$

Standard: Specify locations and describe spatial relationships using coordinate geometry and other representational systems

Expectation: Use Cartesian coordinates and other coordinate systems to analyze geometric situations

A ship travels due south for 40 miles and then southwest for 30 miles. Which of the vectors in the figure below best represents the result of the ship's movement from its starting point? Justify your answer.

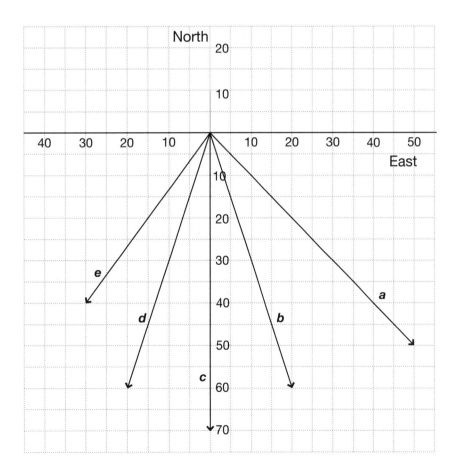

Source: Adapted from *Results from the Seventh Mathematics Assessment of the National Assessment of Educational Progress* (Silver and Kenney 2000)
About the mathematics: This problem provides an excellent context for vectors and visual understandings. It allows students to demonstrate their understanding of the properties of vectors and how we use the Cartesian plane to represent vectors. Students then must communicate their mathematical thinking to others.

Solution: Vector *d*

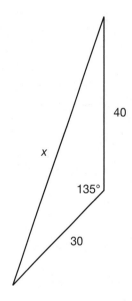

$$x = \sqrt{40^2 + 30^2 - 2(40)(30)\cos(135°)} \approx 64.8$$

$$\vec{d} = \sqrt{20^2 + 60^2} \approx 63.2$$

Standard: Analyze characteristics and properties of two- and three-dimensional geometric shapes and develop mathematical arguments about geometric relationships

Expectations: (a) Analyze properties and determine attributes of two- and three-dimensional objects; (b) explore relationships (including congruence and similarity) among geometric objects, make and test conjectures about them, and solve problems involving them

5

In the figure below, $\overline{AB} \parallel \overline{DE}$ and $\overline{DF} \perp \overline{CE}$. Determine the perimeter of $\triangle CDE$. Explain completely how you found your answers and how you know they are correct.

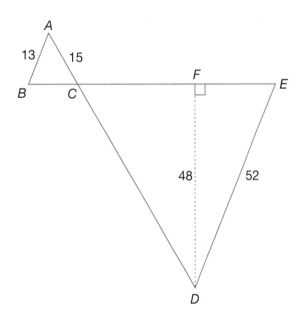

Source: *Principles and Standards for School Mathematics* (NCTM 2000, p. 310, fig. 7.12)

About the mathematics: Although several different approaches are possible, students must know a lot of geometry as well as the Pythagorean theorem to solve the problem. The item allows students to demonstrate their understanding of similar triangles and of scale factor and its relationship to area and perimeter. Students are also given an opportunity to organize their reasoning and consolidate their mathematical thinking through communication.

Solution

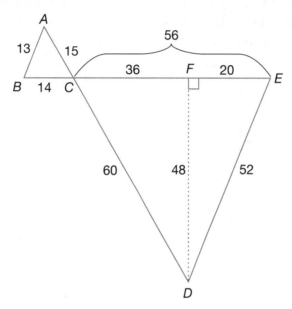

Since $\angle ACB \cong \angle DCE$ (vertical angles are $\cong$) and $\angle ABC \cong \angle DEC$ (parallel lines cut by transversal, alternate interior angles are $\cong$), then $\triangle ABC \sim \triangle DEC$ (A.A. $\sim$). Therefore,

$$\frac{AB}{DE} = \frac{AC}{DC};$$

or by substituting,

$$\frac{13}{52} = \frac{15}{DC} \Rightarrow DC = 60,$$

$$EF = \sqrt{52^2 - 48^2} = 20,$$

$$FC = \sqrt{60^2 - 48^2} = 36,$$

$$CE = CF + FG = 36 + 20 = 56,$$

$$\frac{AB}{DE} = \frac{BC}{EC};$$

or by substituting,

$$\frac{13}{52} = \frac{BC}{56} \Rightarrow BC = 14.$$

Perimeter $\triangle CDE = 56 + 60 + 52 = 168$.

Perimeter $\triangle ABC = 13 + 14 + 15 = 42$.

Since $\triangle ABC \sim \triangle DEC$ and their scale factor is $^1/_4$, the ratio of their perimeters must also be $^1/_4$; $^{42}/_{168} = ^1/_4$.

Student Work

Student A

Student A's work represents the typical student response.

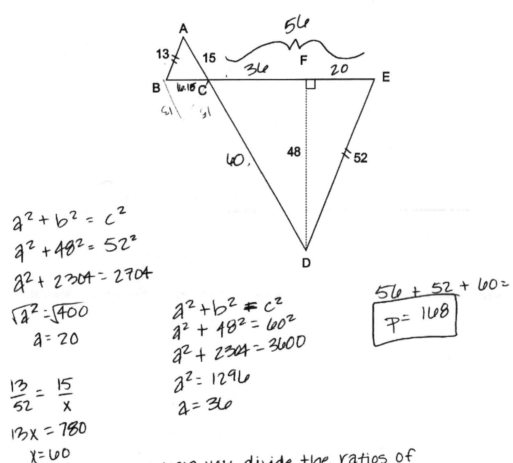

Student B

Student B found the perimeter but did not explain how he knew he was correct by looking at the ratio of sides to the ratio of perimeters. Students are accustomed to just getting an answer and stopping. They need to understand how to best justify their answers.

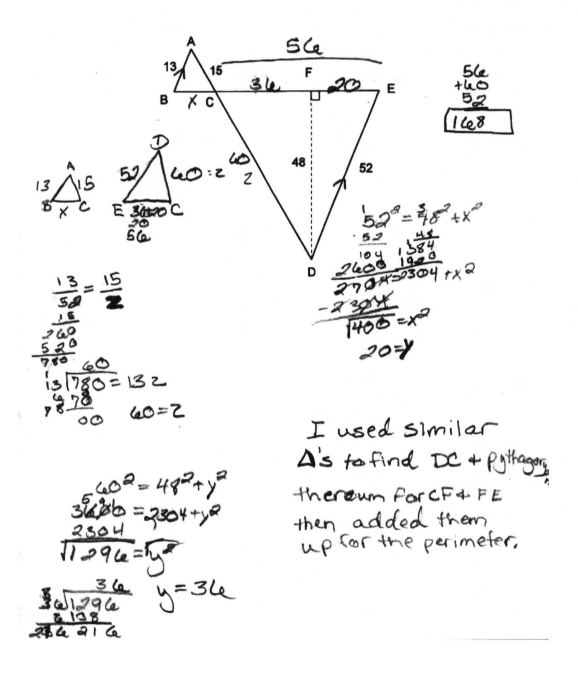

I used similar $\triangle$'s to find DC + Pythagorean theorem for CF + FE then added them up for the perimeter.

Standard: Analyze characteristics and properties of two- and three-dimensional geometric shapes and develop mathematical arguments about geometric relationships

Expectation: Establish the validity of geometric conjectures using deduction and proofs

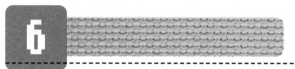

In triangle *ABC* below, the altitudes *BN* and *CM* intersect at point *S*. The measure of angle *MSB* is 40°, and the measure of angle *SBC* is 20°. Write a *proof* of the following statement: "Triangle *ABC* is isosceles."

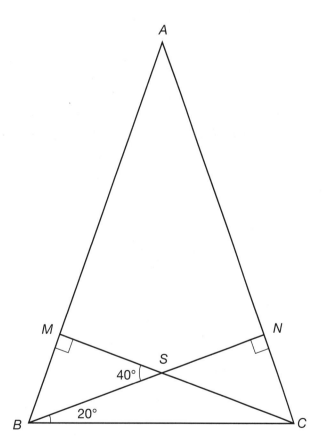

Source: Adapted from TIMSS Population 3 Item Pool (K-18)

About the mathematics: This item allows students to demonstrate their understanding of the many definitions, postulates, and theorems presented in a formal geometry course to prove a statement from a given set of information. Students may use any form of a formal proof, but they need to justify each statement in their proof. This problem can also be used to emphasize the importance of structured solutions and logical reasoning in mathematics. This problem illustrates NCTM's statements concerning proof: "(Students) should be able to produce logical arguments and present formal proofs that effectively explain their reasoning, whether in paragraph, two-column, or some other form of proof." (NCTM 2000, p. 345)

Solution

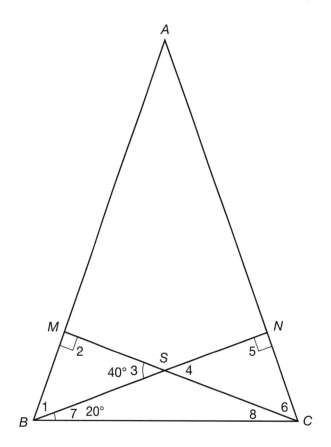

Statements	Reasons
1. $\overline{BN}$ and $\overline{CM}$ are altitudes of $\triangle ABC$, $m\angle MSB = 40°$, $m\angle SBC = 20°$	1. Given
2. $m\angle MSB = m\angle SBC + m\angle SCB$	2. Measure of an exterior angle equals the sum of the measures of the remote interior angles
3. $40° = 20° + m\angle SCB$	3. Substitution
4. $20° = m\angle SCB$	4. Addition/subtraction property of equality
5. $m\angle SCB = m\angle SBC$	5. Transitive property of equality
6. $\angle SCB \cong \angle SBC$	6. Definition of congruent angles
7. $\overline{BC} \cong \overline{BC}$	7. Reflexive property of congruence
8. $\overline{CM} \perp \overline{AB}, \overline{BN} \perp \overline{AC}$	8. Definition of altitude
9. $\angle CMB$ and $\angle BNC$ are right angles	9. Definition of perpendicular
10. $\angle CMB \cong \angle BNC$	10. All right angles are congruent
11. $\triangle CMB \cong \triangle BNC$	11. AAS
12. $\angle ABC \cong \angle ACB$	12. Corresponding parts of congruent triangles are congruent
13. $\overline{AB} \cong \overline{AC}$	13. If two angles of a triangle are congruent, then the sides opposite those angles are congruent
14. $\triangle ABC$ is isosceles	14. Definition of isosceles triangle

Teacher note: Additional samples of student work on the proof problem can be found in chapter 6, "Professional Development."

Student Work

Student A

This solution is the closest to a complete proof that we obtained for this item from all the students in the pilot test. The major difficulty for this student is with step (j). The sum of the angles should be 180, not 360. This mistake affected steps (k), (l), and (m). She also took a very long route to a proof.

Given: $\overline{BN}$ and $\overline{CM}$ are altitudes of $\triangle ABC$ and they intersect at point S
$m\angle MSB = 40°$, $m\angle SBC = 20°$

Prove: Triangle ABC is isosceles

statements	Reasons
a) $m\angle MSB = 40°$ $\overline{BN}$ and $\overline{CM}$ are altitudes of $\triangle ABC$ $m\angle SBC = 20°$	a) Given
b) $\angle MSB$ and $\angle NSC$ are vertical angles	b) Definition of Vertical Angles
c) $\angle MSB$ and $\angle NSC$ are $\cong$	c) Vertical $\angle$'s are $\cong$
d) $m\angle MSB = m\angle NSC$	d) Def. congruency
e) $m\angle MSB = 40°$	e) Given
f) $m\angle NSC = 40°$	f) Transitive prop. of equality
g) $\overline{BN}$ is $\perp$ to $\overline{AC}$ $\overline{CM}$ is $\perp$ to $\overline{AB}$	g) Def. altitudes
h) $\angle SNC$ is a right angle $\angle SMB$ is a right angle	h) Def. $\perp$ lines
i) $m\angle SNC = 90°$, $m\angle SMB = 90°$	i) Def right angles
j) $m\angle SNC + m\angle NSC + m\angle NCS = 360°$ $m\angle MSB + m\angle SMB + m\angle MBS = 360°$	j) Def of $\triangle$
k) $90 + 40 + m\angle NCS = 360°$ $40 + 40 + m\angle MBS = 360°$	k) substitution Property of Equality
l) $130 + m\angle NCS = 360°$ $130 + m\angle MBS = 360$	l) Addition Property of Equality
m) $m\angle NCS = 230$, $m\angle MBS = 230$	m) Subtraction Prop of Equality
n) $m\angle NCS = m\angle MBS$	n) substitution Prop. of (=)

(Continued on page 91)

(Continued from page 90)

statements	Reasons
o) $m\angle MsB = m\angle SBC + m\angle SCB$	o) The measure of an exterior angle of a triangle is equal the sum of the remote interior angles.
p) $40 = 20 + m\angle SCB$	p) Substitution Prop. of (=)
q) $20 = m\angle SCB$	q) Subtraction Prop. of (=)
r) $m\angle SCB = m\angle SBC$	r) Transitive Prop. of (=)
s) $m\angle ABC = m\angle MBS + m\angle SBC$ $m\angle ACB = m\angle NCS + m\angle SCB$	s) Angle Addition Postulate
t) $m\angle ABC = m\angle NCS + m\angle SCB$ $m\angle ACB = m\angle MBS + m\angle SBC$	t) Substitution Prop. of (=)
u) $m\angle ABC = m\angle ACB$	u) Transitive Prop. of (=)
v) $\angle ABC \cong \angle ACB$	v) Def. of congruence
w) $\overline{AB} \cong \overline{AC}$	w) If two angles of a $\triangle$ are congruent, then the sides opposite are $\cong$
x) Triangle ABC is isosceles	x) Def. of isosceles $\triangle$

Standard: Apply transformations and use symmetry to analyze mathematical situations

Expectation: Understand and represent translations, reflections, rotations, and dilations of objects in the plane by using sketches, coordinates, vectors, function notation, and matrices

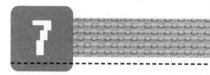

Consider a triangle ABC with vertices $A(-5, 1)$, $B(-4, 7)$, and $C(-8, 5)$. Reflect the triangle over the line $y = x$ to obtain the triangle $A'B'C'$, as shown below.

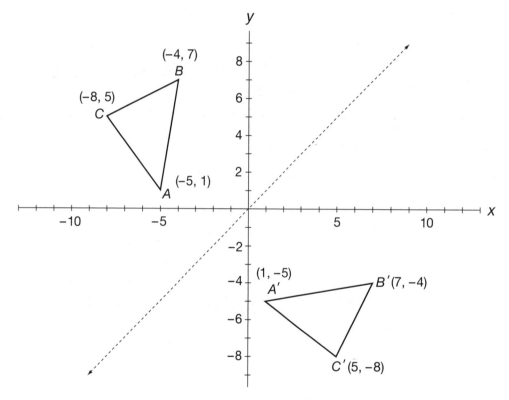

Determine a matrix M such that $MA = A'$, $MB = B'$, and $MC = C'$.

Source: *Principles and Standards for School Mathematics* (NCTM 2000, p. 315, fig. 7.17)

About the mathematics: This problem illustrates a good use of matrices and transformations and the relationship between them. It allows students to demonstrate their understanding of the relationship between geometric figures placed on a coordinate plane and how matrices can be used to transform the figures to a new position on the plane. Students can find the required matrix using the method of their choice.

Solution

$$\overset{M}{\begin{bmatrix} a & b \\ c & d \end{bmatrix}} \begin{bmatrix} -5 & -4 & -8 \\ 1 & 7 & 5 \end{bmatrix} = \begin{bmatrix} 1 & 7 & 5 \\ -5 & -4 & -8 \end{bmatrix}$$

$2 \times 2 \quad 2 \times 3 \qquad 2 \times 3$

$$-5a + b = 1$$

$$\begin{aligned} -4a + 7b &= 7 \\ -4a + 7 &= 7 \\ -4a &= 0 \\ a &= 0 \end{aligned}$$

$$\begin{aligned} -8a + 5b &= 5 \\ 8a - 14b &= -14 \\ -9b &= -9 \\ b &= 1 \end{aligned}$$

$$-5c + d = -5$$

$$\begin{aligned} -4c + 7d &= -4 \\ -4c + 7(0) &= -4 \\ -4c &= -4 \\ c &= 1 \end{aligned}$$

$$\begin{aligned} -8c + 5d &= -8 \\ 8c - 14d &= 8 \\ -9d &= 0 \\ d &= 0 \end{aligned}$$

$$M = \begin{bmatrix} a & b \\ c & d \end{bmatrix} = \begin{bmatrix} 0 & 1 \\ 1 & 0 \end{bmatrix}$$

Standard: Analyze characteristics and properties of two- and three-dimensional geometric shapes and develop mathematical arguments about geometric relationships

Expectation: (a) Analyze properties and determine attributes of two- and three-dimensional objects; (b) explore relationships (including congruence and similarity) among geometric objects, make and test conjectures about them, and solve problems involving them

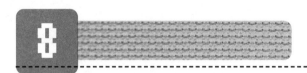

Two marbles are sitting side by side in a glass container. The base of the container is 10 units in length, and the radius of the smaller marble is 2 units.

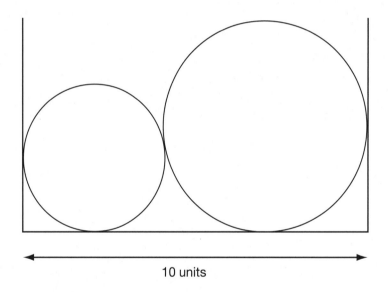

10 units

a. Describe a strategy that you could use to find the radius of the large marble.
b. Use this strategy to calculate the radius of the large marble.

About the mathematics: This problem requires students to find several relationships. They must create figures by drawing lines and finding measurements. Although the problem is easy to understand, it is not easy to solve. It allows students to demonstrate their understanding of the relationship between geometric figures and requires that students know the properties of circles and have an understanding of tangency.

Solution

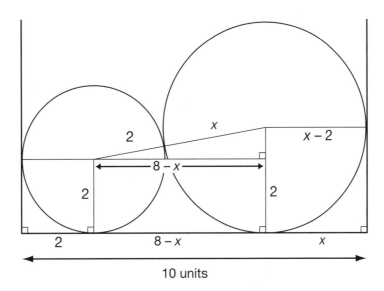

10 units

Using the Pythagorean theorem with the lengths of the segments connecting the centers and the legs of the right triangle, we have the following:

$$(8-x)^2 + (x-2)^2 = (x+2)^2$$
$$64 - 16x + x^2 + x^2 - 4x + 4 = x^2 + 4x + 4$$
$$2x^2 - 20x + 68 = x^2 + 4x + 4$$
$$x^2 - 24x + 64 = 0$$
$$x = 12 \pm 4\sqrt{5}$$

(Discard $x = 12 + 4\sqrt{5}$.) The radius of the larger marble is $x = 12 - 4\sqrt{5}$, or approximately 3.06 units.

Student Work

Student A

Student A was among the very few students who were able to answer this problem correctly.

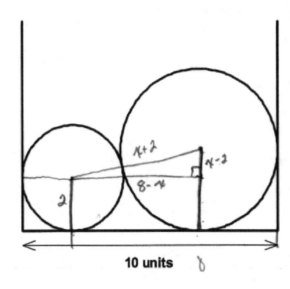

a. Describe a strategy that you could use to find the radius of the large marble.

Pythagorean therm & solve for x

b. Use this strategy to calculate the radius of the large marble.

$$(8-x)^2 + (x-2)^2 = (x+2)^2$$

$$64 - 16x + x^2 + x^2 - 4x + 4 = x^2 + 4x + 4$$

$$x^2 - 24x + 64 = 0$$

$$x = 3.06$$

Student B

This solution was the most commonly used incorrect approach.

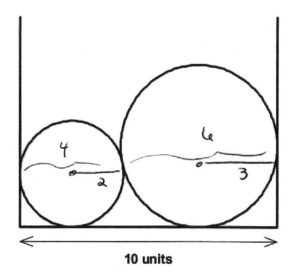

10 units

a. Describe a strategy that you could use to find the radius of the large marble.

Double the radius of the smaller marble to get 4 units. Subtract 4 from the base length to get 6 units for the big marble. Divide 6 by 2 to get the big marbles radius, 3 units.

b. Use this strategy to calculate the radius of the large marble.

3 units

Standard: Analyze characteristics and properties of two- and three-dimensional geometric shapes and develop mathematical arguments about geometric relationships

Expectation: Analyze properties and determine attributes of two- and three-dimensional objects

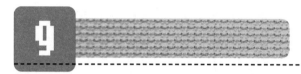

A star is made by cutting quarter circles from a square sheet of cardboard with sides of length *L,* as shown.

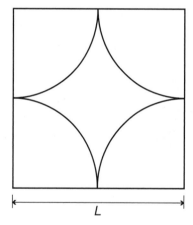

L

a. Write an expression for the area of the star as a function of side length *L.*
b. About what fraction of the area of the square was cut away to make the star?
c. Does the answer to part *b* depend on the length *L?* Explain.
d. How far could a bug walk along the edge of the star, without retracing its path, before returning to its starting point?
e. Does the answer to part *d* depend on the length *L?* Explain.

Source: Adapted from *Balanced Assessment for the Mathematics Curriculum* (Schwartz and Kenney 2000, p. 29, BA 18-02, problem HS034). These tasks were developed with the support of the National Science Foundation. Copyright © 1995–2000 by President and Fellows of Maryland College. All rights reserved. Used with permission.

About the mathematics: This item allows students to demonstrate their understanding of area, perimeter of a square, and circumference of a circle. Students will need to explain how changing a single dimension, the length of the side of the square, affects the area and perimeter of the square and the area and circumference of the circle.

Solution

a. Write an expression for the area (A) of the star as a function of side length L.

$$A(L) = L^2 - \pi \left(\frac{L}{2}\right)^2 = L^2 - \frac{\pi}{4}L^2$$

b. About what fraction of the area of the square was cut away to make the star?

$$\frac{\pi}{4} \approx 0.785,$$

or a little over $3/4$.

c. Does the answer to part b depend on the length L? Explain.

$$\frac{A_{circle}}{A_{square}} = \frac{\frac{\pi}{4}L^2}{L^2} = \frac{\pi}{4}$$

No, the amount cut away will always be $\pi/4$. Since π is a constant, the length of L does not matter.

d. How far could a bug walk along the edge of the star, without retracing its path, before returning to its starting point?

$$2\pi \left(\frac{L}{2}\right) = \pi L$$

e. Does the answer to part d depend on the length L? Explain.
   Yes. When calculating πL, as L gets larger, the distance the bug walks is longer.

Student Work

Student A

The student needs to explain how she got this answer. It appears that the student does not understand that the answers to parts c and e should reflect and use the answers from parts b and d. In part a, the student has inappropriately placed π in parentheses. Whether this placement is a careless error or signals a misconception is impossible to determine.

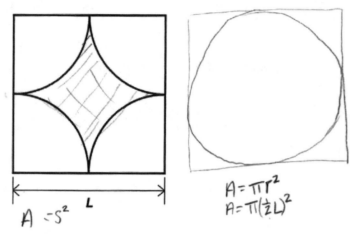

$A = s^2$ L

$A = \pi r^2$
$A = \pi (\tfrac{1}{2} L)^2$

a. Write an expression for the area of the star as a function of side length L.

$$A = L^2 - \left(\pi \tfrac{L}{2}\right)^2$$

b. About what fraction of the area of the square was cut away in order to make the star?

$$\frac{4}{5}$$

c. Does the answer to part b depend upon the length L? Explain.

No because in order to create the stars then the sides of the quarters circles need to touch making them bigger in proportion to the square.

d. How far could a bug walk along the edge of the star, without retracing its path, before returning to its starting point?

$$C = 2\pi r$$
$$C = 2\pi\left(\tfrac{L}{2}\right)$$

e. Does the answer to part d depend upon the length L? Explain.

yes because if length L is larger then the bug would have to walk farther to get around the circle.

Student B

The student made the common mistake of simplifying $\left(\dfrac{l}{2}\right)^2$ as $\dfrac{l^2}{2}$. The student should relate the answer for part e to the answer in part d.

    a. Write an expression for the area of the star as a function of side length L.

$$A = l^2 - \pi \frac{l}{2}^2$$

    b. About what fraction of the area of the square was cut away in order to make the star?

$$3/4$$

    c. Does the answer to part b depend upon the length L? Explain.

no, no matter what the value of L is, the fraction will remain the same

    d. How far could a bug walk along the edge of the star, without retracing its path, before returning to its starting point?

$$2\pi \frac{L}{2}$$

    e. Does the answer to part d depend upon the length L? Explain.

yes, because if the value of L is different the distance the bug walked would change

Student C

How the student came up with her expression for area is difficult to understand. She should be interviewed and asked to explain her reasoning so that the teacher can help clear up her misunderstandings. Confusing the formulas for area and circumference of circles, as this student did in part d, was a commonly made mistake by students.

a. Write an expression for the area of the star as a function of side length L.

$$2 \cdot L - \tfrac{3}{4} \, \pi (\tfrac{1}{2} L)^2 = \text{area of star or square } -$$
area of ○ with radius of ½L

b. About what fraction of the area of the square was cut away in order to make the star?

$$\frac{\text{area of star}}{\text{area of square}}$$

c. Does the answer to part b depend upon the length L? Explain.

NO. due to the fact that the prop. will stay the same no matter the length of L.

d. How far could a bug walk along the edge of the star, without retracing its path, before returning to its starting point?

$$\pi r^2 \text{ or the circumference of the } ○$$
with the radius of ½L

e. Does the answer to part d depend upon the length L? Explain.

Yes. due to the fact that the circumference, or should say each quarter of its circumference, is proportional to the length of L.

Standard: Use visualization, spatial reasoning, and geometric modeling to solve problems

Expectation: Draw and construct representations of two- and three-dimensional geometric objects using a variety of tools

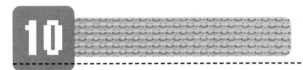

The diameter of the given circle is the same length as the side of the given square. For each of the shapes below, use your geometry tools to construct a figure that has exactly the same shape and whose—

a. perimeter/circumference is twice as long;
b. area is twice as large.

In each instance, explain your reasoning.

This problem is cross-listed with chapter 4, "Measurement." The sections "About the mathematics," "Solution," and "Student Work" are contained in that chapter.

Standard: Analyze characteristics and properties of two- and three-dimensional geometric shapes and develop mathematical arguments about geometric relationships

Expectation: Explore relationships among classes of two- and three-dimensional objects and solve problems involving them

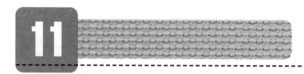

Use the grid below to answer the questions. Show as much of your work as possible. Sketch a smaller square inside the given square so that the smaller square is half the area of the larger square. Write an explanation to convince another person that your new, smaller square is truly half the area of the original square.

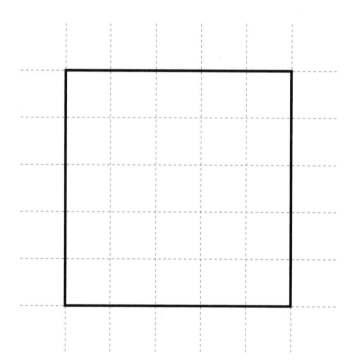

This problem is cross-listed with chapter 5, "Measurement." The sections "About the Mathematics," "Solution," and "Student Work" are contained in that chapter.

Standard: Analyze characteristics and properties of two- and three-dimensional geometric shapes and develop mathematical arguments about geometric relationships

Expectation: Explore relationships among classes of two- and three-dimensional objects and solve problems involving them

Standard: Use visualization, spatial reasoning, and geometric modeling to solve problems

Expectation: Visualize three-dimensional objects from different perspectives and analyze their cross-sections

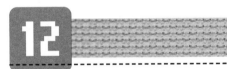

The dimensions of a small house are 12 meters long, 12 meters wide, and 3 meters tall. The roof forms a pyramid with all edges measuring 12 meters. An extra room is needed, so your job is to design an attic room, inscribed in the pyramid, that has the same length, width, and height.

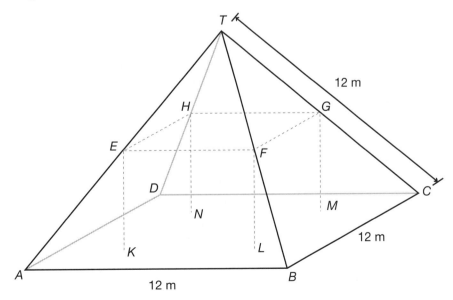

a. What are the length, width, and height of the room you designed?

b. Is the attic room taller or shorter than the downstairs rooms?

c. Do these dimensions seem appropriate for a room, or should the plan be revised? Explain your response.

d. The space behind the four walls of the new room can be used as storage. What is the volume of this storage space?

> This problem is cross-listed with chapter 4, "Measurement." The sections "About the mathematics," "Solution," and "Student Work" are contained in that chapter.

Challenger

Standard: Analyze characteristics and properties of two- and three-dimensional geometric shapes and develop mathematical arguments about geometric relationships

Expectation: Explore relationships among classes of two- and three-dimensional objects and solve problems involving them

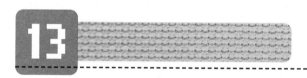

What is the geometric probability that two positive numbers, x and y (both less than 1), written down at random, together with the number 1, yield a trio of numbers $(x, y, 1)$ that are the sides of an obtuse-angled triangle?

> **Source:** *Ingenuity in Mathematics* (Honsberger 1970, p. 4). All rights reserved. Used with permission.
>
> **About the mathematics:** Students must begin by understanding the relationships among the sides of a triangle, knowing the law of cosines, and knowing the value of cosine in quadrant II because the angle is obtuse. By combining this knowledge with that of the relationship between area and probability, students are able to arrive at a solution. These connections are difficult for many students, thus creating a challenging problem rich in mathematics and problem solving.

Solution

Because *x* and *y* are both less than 1, they determine a point $P(x, y)$ in the unit square. Consider a triangle with sides, *x*, *y*, and 1.

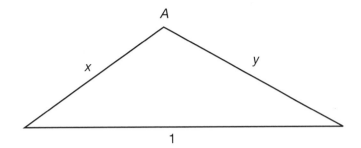

We know that $1 + x > y$ and $1 + y > x$, because the sum of any two of them must exceed the third if they form any type of triangle. Therefore $x + y > 1$. We apply the law of cosines to the triangle to get

$$1^2 = x^2 + y^2 - 2xy \cdot \cos A$$

or

$$x^2 + y^2 = 1 + 2xy \cdot \cos A.$$

Because 1 is the longest side, then $\angle A$ must be the largest angle. If $\angle A$ is obtuse, then cos *A* must be negative. Hence the condition that the triangle is obtuse is $x^2 + y^2 < 1$. Putting this condition with $x + y > 1$, we know the point $P(x, y)$ must lie in the shaded segment below.

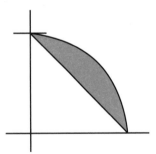

The area of the quarter-circle with radius 1 is

$$\frac{\pi}{4},$$

and the area of the triangle is

$$\frac{1}{2}.$$

Therefore, the geometric probability is the ratio of the area of the shaded part to the area of the square, which is

$$\frac{\pi}{4} - \frac{1}{2}$$

because the area of the square is 1.

Measurement

STANDARDS and student Expectations for measurement from *Principles and Standards for School Mathematics* (NCTM 2000) are reflected in the items included in this chapter. The items focus on problem situations involving measurement techniques, the understanding and application of standard measurement formulas, and the use of unit analysis to solve problems and check solutions. Students are required to work problems that demonstrate how measurement can be affected by their choice of units and scale factors. Students are also required to solve problems with nonlinear scale changes and explain how these techniques can be used in analyzing measurement data.

Because the application of measurement arises naturally in other areas of mathematics, four of the six problems in this chapter are cross-listed with other chapters. Some of the problems could be used as in-class, structured activities or as group projects. The items address the Process Standards of Problem Solving, Reasoning and Proof, Communications, Connections, and Representation.

The student work in the chapter illustrates some common misconceptions and misunderstandings that students have about measurement, especially scale factors and dimensional analysis.

Measurement Assessment Items

Standard: Understand measurable attributes of objects and the units, systems, and processes of measurement

Expectation: Make decisions about units and scales that are appropriate for problem situations involving measurement

Standard: Apply appropriate techniques, tools, and formulas to determine measurements

Expectation: Use unit analysis to check measurement computations

You are headed to Canada, and you need to know how many hours the drive from Calgary, Alberta, to Edmonton, Alberta, will take. The only distance you are able to find between these two cities is 294 kilometers.

a. If speed limits in Canada are comparable to speed limits in the United States and you usually average 60 miles per hour when traveling, how many hours will the trip take?

b. Your car averages 26 miles per gallon. How many liters of fuel will you need for the trip? (Fuel in Canada is sold in liters.)

c. Fuel prices in the United States are approximately $2.75 per gallon in comparison with fuel prices in Canada, which are approximately $1.04 Canadian dollars per liter. United States prices are given in United States dollars, and Canadian prices are given in Canadian dollars. Where would it cost less to travel the 294 kilometers, the United States or Canada?

Conversions you may need for this problem are the following:

$$1 \text{ kilometer} = .6214 \text{ miles}$$
$$1 \text{ gallon} = 3.785 \text{ liters}$$
$$1 \text{ U.S. dollar} = 1.3264 \text{ Canadian dollars}$$

About the mathematics: This problem allows students to work with a real-life problem that involves conversions. It also requires them to demonstrate their proficiency in dimensional analysis, thus connecting well with the types of problems that students often encounter in their science classes.

Solution

a. $\dfrac{60 \text{ miles}}{1 \text{ hour}} \cdot \dfrac{1 \text{ kilometer}}{0.6214 \text{ miles}} = 96.556 \text{ kilometers per hour}$

294 kilometers ÷ 96.556 kilometers per hour = 3.04486 hours

b. $\dfrac{1 \text{ gal}}{26 \text{ miles}} \cdot \dfrac{3.785 \text{ liters}}{1 \text{ gal}} \cdot \dfrac{0.6214 \text{ miles}}{1 \text{ kilometer}} \cdot 294 \text{ kilometers} \approx 26.6 \text{ liters}$

c. $\dfrac{2.75 \text{ U.S. dollars}}{1 \text{ gallon}} \cdot \dfrac{1 \text{ gallon}}{3.785 \text{ liters}} \cdot \dfrac{1.3264 \text{ Canadian dollars}}{1 \text{ U.S. dollars}}$

≈ 96.3 Canadian cents per liter

Traveling the 294 kilometers would be less expensive in the United States because fuel would cost 96.3 Canadian cents per liter instead of 104.1 Canadian cents, or $1.04 Canadian, per liter.

Standard: Apply appropriate techniques, tools, and formulas to determine measurements

Expectation: Understand and use formulas for area and perimeter of geometric figures

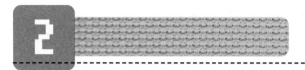

The diameter of the given circle is the same length as the side of the given square. For each of the shapes below, use your geometry tools and construct a figure that has exactly the same shape and whose—

a. perimeter/circumference is twice as long;
b. area is twice as large.

In each instance, explain your reasoning.

Source: Adapted from *Balanced Assessment for the Twenty-first Century* (Schwartz and Kenney 2000, p. 93, problem HS033). These tasks were developed with the support of the National Science Foundation. Copyright © 1995–2000 by President and Fellows of Maryland College. All rights reserved. Used with permission.

About the mathematics: This item allows students to demonstrate their understanding of perimeter and area when they are not given an actual length of a side or the radius of a circle. Students may approach the problem in various ways and at various levels of understanding. A student might simply use a trial-and-error approach by trying various lengths of sides and radii until finding the correct perimeter or area. A more advanced understanding might incorporate the use of scale factor and how it relates to perimeter and area. The structured problem is a good in-class activity. If it is too difficult for students, the center of the circle could be given.

Solution

a. Double the length of the side or radius of the original figure.
b. Take $\sqrt{2}$ times the length of the side or radius of the original figure.

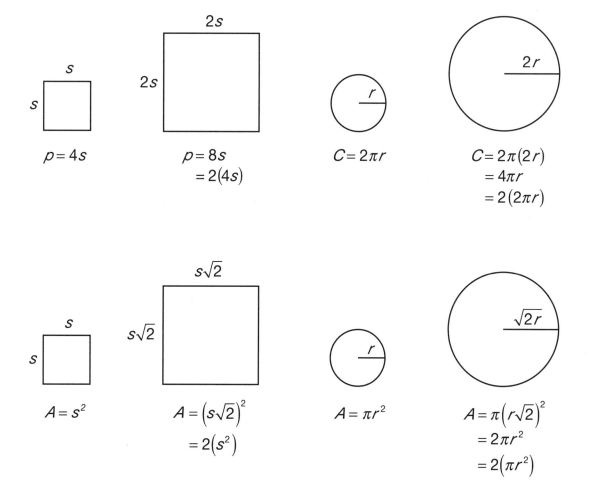

Student Work

All the student work shown here illustrates a misunderstanding about dimensional analysis and scale factors. Students were erroneously operating under the assumption that if the sides or radius doubled, both the perimeter and the area also doubled.

Student A

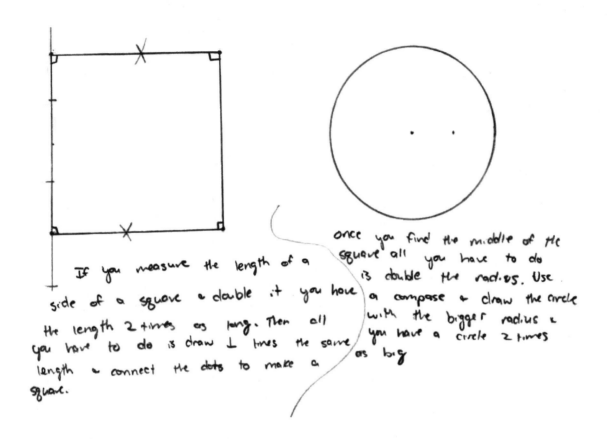

If you measure the length of a side of a square & double it you have the length 2 times as long. Then all you have to do is draw ⊥ times the same length & connect the dots to make a square.

once you find the middle of the square all you have to do is double the radius. Use a compass & draw the circle with the bigger radius & you have a circle 2 times as big

Student B

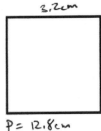

3.2cm

P= 12.8cm
A= 10.24 cm

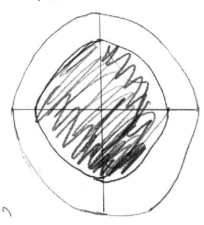

5.2 cm

$\pi(1.6)^2$

Area = 8.04 cm

C = 2 $\pi(1.6)$ =
   C = 10.05 cm

(Pretend I can draw a circle)

In each case, explain your reasoning.

6.4

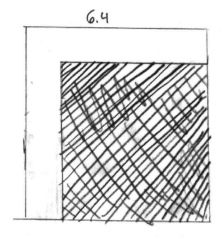

P = 25.6 cm
A = 20.48 cm

A = 16.08 cm
C = 20.1 cm

On both Shapes the perimeter/circumference of the shape is twice as long and the area of the shaded region is twice as large

Student C

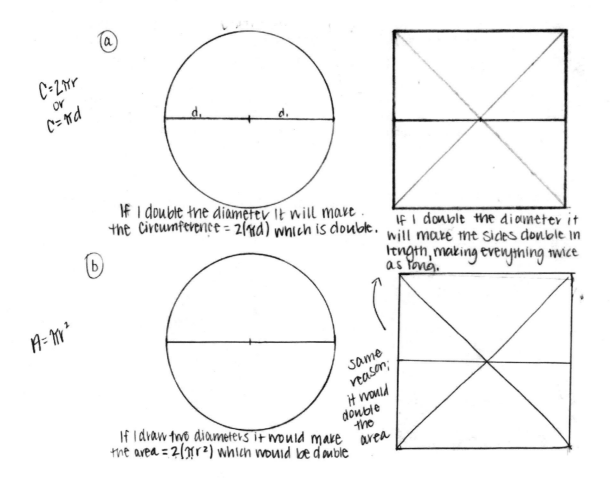

ⓐ

$C = 2\pi r$
or
$C = \pi d$

d, · d,

If I double the diameter it will make
the Circumference = $2(\pi d)$ which is double.

If I double the diameter it
will make the sides double in
length, making everything twice
as long.

ⓑ

$A = \pi r^2$

If I draw two diameters it would make
the area = $2(\pi r^2)$ which would be double

same
reason;
it would
double
the
area

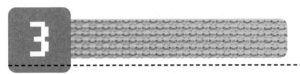

A star is made by cutting quarter circles from a square sheet of cardboard with sides of length *L,* as shown.

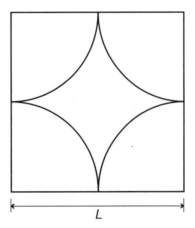

L

a. Write an expression for the area of the star as a function of side length *L.*
b. About what fraction of the area of the square was cut away to make the star?
c. Does the answer to part b depend on length *L?* Explain.
d. How far could a bug walk along the edge of the star, without retracing its path, before returning to its starting point?
e. Does the answer to part d depend on length *L?* Explain.

Source: *Balanced Assessment for the Mathematics Curriculum* (2002, p. 29, BA 18-02, problem HS034). These tasks were developed with the support of the National Science Foundation. Copyright © 1995–2000 by President and Fellows of Maryland College. All rights reserved. Used with permission.

Problem 3 is cross-listed with chapter 3, "Geometry." The sections on "About the mathematics," "Solution," and "Student Work" are contained in that chapter.

Standard: Understand measurable attributes of objects and the units, systems, and processes of measurement

Expectation: Make decisions about units and scales that are appropriate for problem situations involving measurement

Standard: Apply appropriate techniques, tools, and formulas to determine measurements

Expectation: Understand and use formulas for area of geometric figures

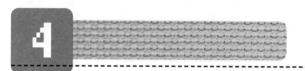

Use the grid below to answer the questions. Show as much of your work as possible. Sketch a smaller square inside the given square so that the smaller square is half the area of the larger square. Write an explanation to convince another person that your new, smaller square is truly half the area of the original square.

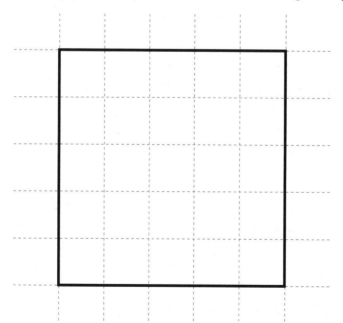

About the mathematics: This item allows students to show their understanding of area and scale factor. Students may approach the problem in various ways and at various levels of understanding. The problem was piloted as a 5 × 5 and later as a 6 × 6 grid so that we could determine whether a difference was found using even- or odd-numbered grids.

Solution: One possible solution is to connect the midpoints of each side of the square. The square formed by connecting these points has half the area of the original square. Verification of solution: If the sides of the square are s, then the area is s^2. To find a square with an area of

$$\frac{s^2}{2},$$

we find the midpoints of each side of the square and connect them. The four triangles formed are 45°-45°-90° right triangles, leaving the figure in the middle a square. The length of the sides of this square is

$$\sqrt{\left(\frac{s}{2}\right)^2 + \left(\frac{s}{2}\right)^2} = \sqrt{\frac{s^2}{4} + \frac{s^2}{4}} = \sqrt{\frac{s^2}{2}} = s\sqrt{\frac{1}{2}} = s\frac{\sqrt{2}}{2}.$$

Hence, the area of the square is

$$\frac{s\sqrt{2}}{2} \cdot \frac{s\sqrt{2}}{2} = \frac{2s^2}{4} = \frac{s^2}{2}.$$

Student Work

Student A

Apparently this student was able to just "see" an approach that worked. The student neglected to support her statement with a mathematical justification.

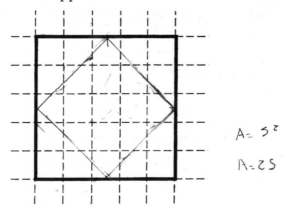

$A = 5^2$

$A = 25$

The area of the big square is 25 and half of that is 12.5 which the small square's area is.

Student B

This student appears to have based his comparison on the ratio of the sides of the squares, making the common error of assuming that doubling (or halving) a side of a square will double (or halve) the area. He gives no specific information about the areas of the squares.

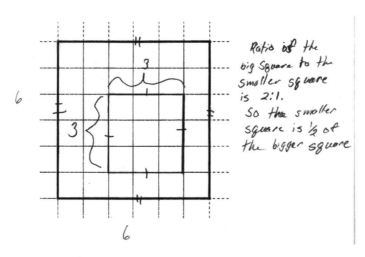

Ratio of the big square to the smaller square is 2:1. So the smaller square is ½ of the bigger square

Student C

This student apparently did not understand the directions, which required students to sketch a square. She did, however, understand that the area of the new figure needed to be 12.5 square units.

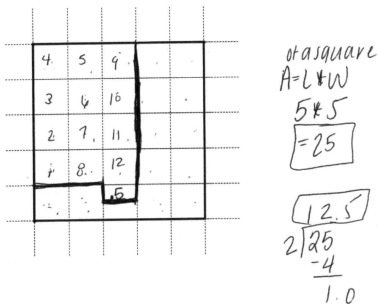

If you take the length and multiply that number by the width and get the area of the square. then you take the total area of the square divide it by two and draw the smaller square with that specific amount of boxes inside the large square.

Additional samples of student work on the grid problems can be found in chapter 6, "Professional Development."

Standard: Apply appropriate techniques, tools, and formulas to determine measurements

Expectation: Understand and use formulas for area and perimeter of geometric figures

5

The dimensions of a small house are 12 meters long, 12 meters wide, and 3 meters tall. The roof forms a pyramid with all edges measuring 12 meters. An extra room is needed, so your job is to design an attic room, inscribed in the pyramid, that has the same length, width, and height.

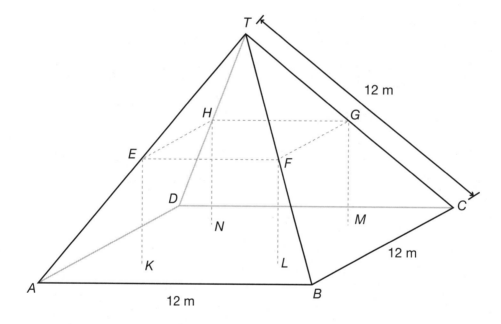

a. What are the length, width, and height of the room you designed?
b. Is the height of the attic room larger or smaller than that of the downstairs rooms?
c. Do these dimensions seem appropriate for a room, or should the plan be revised? Explain your response.
d. The space behind the four walls of the new room can be used as storage. What is the volume of this storage space?

Source: Adapted from *Preparing Students for PISA: Mathematical Literacy* (Nova Scotia Department of Education 2002, p. 23)

About the mathematics: This item allows students to analyze properties and determine the attributes of three-dimensional objects to solve problems that involve drawing or constructing representations of these objects. It also involves a concrete application of constructing a cube inside a pyramid as a room in an attic. The questions about the reasonableness of answers promote good class discussions because students must think about the practicality of their solutions.

Solution

a. Using $\triangle AEK$, let $EK = x$, which represents the length, width, and height of the room. Knowing that all sides of the pyramid are 12 meters, we can let $AE = 12 - x$ and let

$$AK = 6\sqrt{2} - \frac{1}{2}x\sqrt{2}.$$

Set up the equation

$$(12 - x)^2 = x^2 + \left(6\sqrt{2} - \frac{1}{2}x\sqrt{2}\right)^2$$

using the Pythagorean theorem. Solve for x, which is equal to $-12 \pm 12\sqrt{2}$ meters. We use only the positive value because we are solving for distance.

b. The house is 3 meters tall compared with $-12 + 12\sqrt{2} \approx 4.97$ meters for the upstairs room. The room in the attic is quite a bit taller.

c. Students should realize that 5 meters is quite high for a room.

d. Find the volume of the pyramid, and subtract the volume of the room.

$$\frac{1}{3}(12)^2 6\sqrt{2} - \left(-12 + 12\sqrt{2}\right)^3 - \frac{1}{3}\left(-12 + 12\sqrt{2}\right)^2 \left(12 - 6\sqrt{2}\right) \approx 256$$

Standard: Understand measurable attributes of objects and the units, systems, and processes of measurement

Expectation: Make decisions about units and scales that are appropriate for problem situations involving measurement

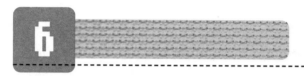

Albert ran across the following graph that showed the variable luminosity of a galactic body observed over a period of several days. He noted that the variability was approximately linear when the time, or horizontal, axis was scaled logarithmically.

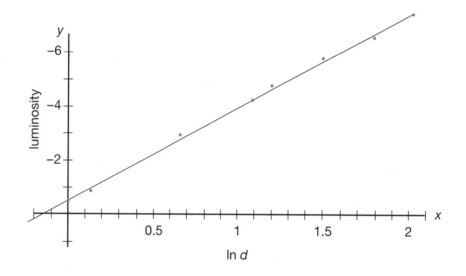

a. At approximately what time, in days (d), would the luminosity be –3?

b. If $y = -3.6x - 0.5$ is the equation of the line predicting luminosity, what is the predicted luminosity after 14 days?

About the mathematics: This problem requires the student to understand the terminology of mathematics and to draw reasonable conclusions about a situation being modeled. Students must also make careful use of the logarithm tics on the horizontal axis to read and interpret the graph. Once they get the information from the graph, students must then convert the abscissa from ln d to d.

Solution

a. Approximately 2 days. On the ln d axis, -3 luminosity corresponds approximately to 0.7:

$$\ln d \approx 0.7$$
$$d \approx 2 \text{ days}$$

b. Predicted luminosity ≈ -10:

$$\ln (14) \approx 2.64$$
$$y = -3.6(2.64) - 0.5 \approx -10$$

Teacher note: For this type of application, physicists often orient the y-axis so that the negative direction is up and the positive is down. Thus, the line in the graph has a negative slope.

Data Analysis and Probability

STANDARDS-based tasks that can be incorporated into teaching data analysis and probability are exemplified in the items in this chapter. These problems give students opportunities to interpret information from graphs to draw conclusions, analyze numerical data and graphs, and use regression models to solve problems. Students must identify characteristics of univariate and bivariate measurement data, find functions that model the data, calculate summary statistics, and develop and evaluate predictions on the basis of data. Problems involving basic concepts of probability, including conditional probability, independent events, and the probability of a compound event, are also included. Students must be able not only to perform these tasks but also to communicate their thinking and justify their answers.

Nine problems are presented in this chapter, including a "challenger" geometric probability problem that is cross-listed with Geometry. Two problems are in multiple-choice format, five require short responses, and two call for extended responses. All problems require a written explanation and justification.

Examples of student work in the chapter illustrate the most common student errors involving probabilities, analysis of data, and conclusions drawn from data.

Data Analysis and Probability Assessment Items

Standard: Understand and apply basic concepts of probability

Expectation: Understand the concepts of conditional probability and independent events; understand how to compute the probability of a compound event

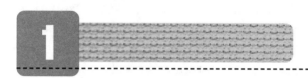

A warning system installation consists of two independent alarms having probabilities of operating in an emergency of 0.95 and 0.90, respectively. Find the probability that at least one alarm operates in an emergency. Show your work.

a. 0.995
b. 0.975
c. 0.95
d. 0.90
e. 0.855

Source: TIMSS Population 3 Item Pool (L-10)

About the mathematics: This problem allows students to solve the problem using a variety of approaches, some more complicated than others. The phrase *at least* gives students the opportunity to show their understanding of the complement of the event that neither of the alarms works.

Solution: a

$$(1 - (0.05)(0.1)) = 1 - 0.005 = 0.995$$

Student Work

Student A

Student A used the general addition rule for the union of two events instead of the complement of the event. An observer can see each step of the rule in the student's work: $P(A \text{ or } B) = P(A) + P(B) - P(A \text{ and } B)$.

a. 0.995
b. 0.975
c. 0.95
d. 0.90
e. 0.855

$$\left(.95 + .9\right) - \left(.95 \cdot .9\right) = .995$$

Student B

Student B based his approach on the use of a Venn diagram. Letting alarm A be one circle and alarm B be the other, the student added the three sections of the diagram to get the correct solution.

a. 0.995
b. 0.975
c. 0.95
d. 0.90
e. 0.855

alarm A   alarm B
.95   .90

both work = .855
A works = .095
B works = .045
       +
0.995 A

$$P(A \cap B) + P(A \cap B^c) + P(A^c \cap B)$$

Student C

Student C made one of the most common errors for this type of problem, perhaps indicating careless reading of the problem or confusion about how to calculate a situation that includes the term *at least*. This solution gives the probability that both alarm 1 and alarm 2 work. It neglects to include the solution for the situation that at least one alarm works.

a. 0.995
b. 0.975
c. 0.95
d. 0.90
e. 0.855

$P(A) = $ Alarm 1 works

$P(B) = $ Alarm 2 works

$$P(A \cup B) = .95 \cdot .90 = .855$$

Standard: Develop and evaluate inferences and predictions that are based on data

Expectation: Understand how sample statistics reflect values of population parameters and use sampling distributions as a basis for informal inference

If the population increases by the same average rate from the year 1990 to the year 2005 as it did in the years from 1975 to 1985, approximately what is the expected population by the year 2005? Justify your answer.

a. 47 million
b. 50 million
c. 53 million
d. 58 million

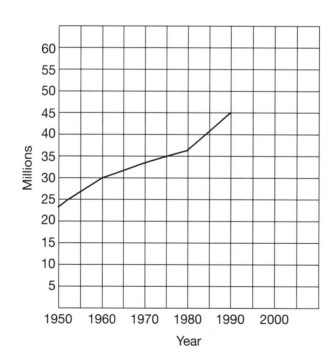

Source: Adapted from TIMSS Population 3 Item Pool (A-4)
About the mathematics: This item allows students to make conjectures about possible relationships between two characteristics of a sample on the basis of a graph. The estimation aspect makes it appropriate for a multiple-choice item. Whether a student saw an increase of 5 or 6 million in the ten-year span does not matter in light of the choices for the solution.
Solution: c

Student Work

Student A

Student A's work indicates that he found the difference between the endpoints of the interval from 1975 to 1985. He then used this difference in a ratio to calculate the rate of change per year. He used the rate of change for one year times the number of years between 1990 and 2005 and added that amount to the value from 1990. He apparently selected the distractor that was closest to his answer.

a. 47 million
b. 50 million
c. 53 million
d. 58 million

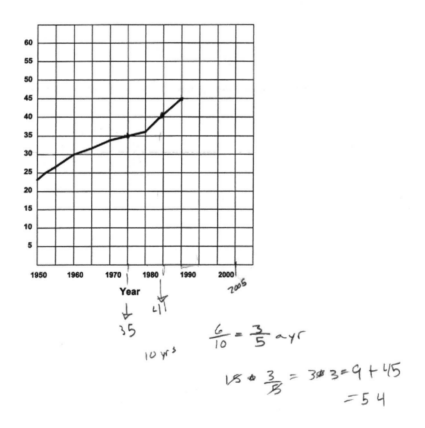

Student B

Student B gave a written explanation. How she calculated the 5 million from 1975 to 1985 is not clear, but she does indicate that the rate for fifteen years will be that 5 million for the first ten years plus half of that 5 million for the change in fifteen years.

a. 47 million
b. 50 million
c. 53 million
d. 58 million

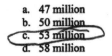

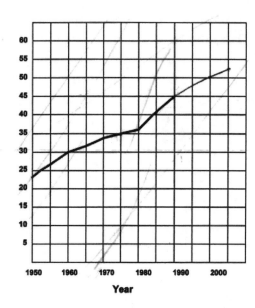

Year

Population ~~was~~ increased 5 million from 1975 to 1985. If the rate remains the same, ~~th~~ the population will increase by 8 million. (5 million in ten years) (~~th~~ 2.5 in 5 years)

Student C

Student C appears to have made a very common error. He calculated the amount of change from 1975 to 1985 as 6 million. He then added that 6 million to the 45 million people represented at (1990, 45), getting a total of 51 million. This student either did not understand the meaning of rate of change or neglected to compensate for the fact that he was asked to calculate the population for an additional fifteen years rather than an additional ten years.

a. 47 million
b. 50 million
c. 53 million
d. 58 million

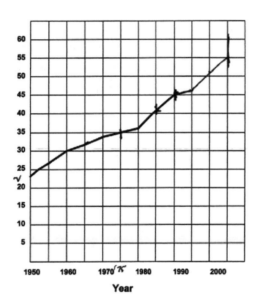

> **Standard:** Develop and evaluate inferences and predictions that are based on data

> **Expectation:** Understand how sample statistics reflect values of population parameters and use sampling distributions as a basis for informal inference

3

Scientists have observed that crickets move their wings faster in warm temperatures than in cold temperatures. By noting the pitch of cricket chirps, one can estimate the air temperature. Below is a graph showing thirteen observations of cricket chirps per second and the associated air temperature.

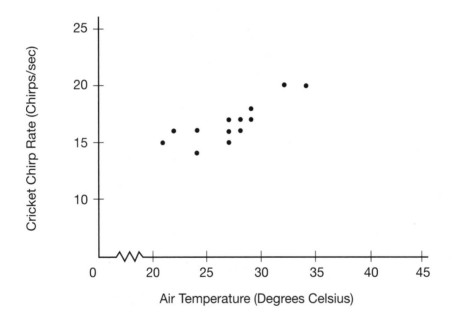

a. On the graph, draw in an estimated line of best fit for these data.
b. Using your line, estimate the number of cricket chirps per second when the air temperature is 30 degrees Celsius.

Source: Adapted from TIMSS Population 3 Item Pool (L-15a)

About the mathematics: This item allows students to make conjectures about possible relationships between two characteristics of a sample on the basis of scatterplots of the data and approximate lines of best fit. The problem is accessible to students with no statistics background if they know how to get an equation of a line. The problem also allows students to recognize and apply mathematics in contexts outside mathematics and use representations to model and interpret physical, social, and mathematical phenomena.

Solution

a. Template for correct lines

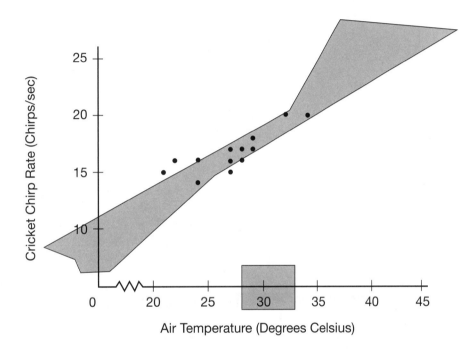

b. 17 chirps per second. But answers may vary because the line of best fit is just an estimate for this problem.

Student Work

Student A

Student A appears to have drawn a line such that it would have half the points above it and half the points below it. This student seems to have used the graph to estimate the number of chirps per second, then written an equation that would result in that number. If the equation is used for other points on the graph, it does not always fit the data given.

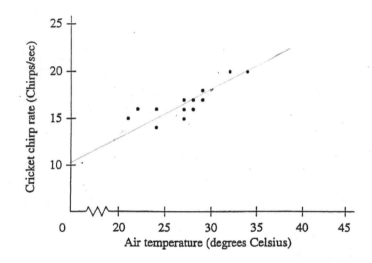

a. On the graph, draw in an estimated line of best fit for these data.

Just approximate trying to get about ½ the points above & ½ below.

b. Using your line, estimate the number of cricket chirps/sec when the air temperature is 30°. ∼ 18

$y = .5X + 3$

Student B

Student B does not give any indication of how he drew the line of best fit. He apparently made an educated guess, fitting the line so that half the points were above the line and half were below. He located the point (30, 17) on the line he had drawn, but we have no way of knowing whether he drew the line first or located the point first.

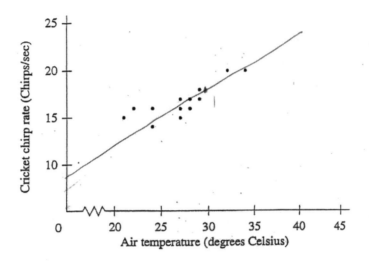

a. On the graph, draw in an estimated line of best fit for these data.

b. Using your line, estimate the number of cricket chirps/sec when the air temperature is 30°.

17 chirps

Standard: Understand and apply basic concepts of probability

Expectations: Understand the concepts of conditional probability and independent events; understand how to compute the probability of a compound event

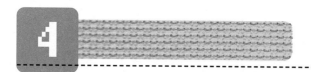

The diagram below shows the results of a two-question survey administered to 80 randomly selected students at Highcrest High School.

Do you play on a
sports team?

		Yes	No
Do you play a musical instrument?	No	32	14
	Yes	14	20

a. Of the 2100 students in the school, how many would you expect to play a musical instrument? Justify your answer.

b. Are playing a musical instrument and playing on a sports team independent events? Justify your answer.

c. Estimate the probability that an arbitrary student at the school plays on a sports team and plays a musical instrument. Justify your answer.

d. Estimate the probability that a student who plays on a sports team also plays a musical instrument. Justify your answer.

Source: Adapted from *Principles and Standards for School Mathematics* (NCTM 2000, pp. 331–32)

About the mathematics: This item allows students to test rules of independent events and solve the problem in different ways. It also allows students to recognize and apply mathematics in contexts outside mathematics and communicate their mathematical thinking to others.

Note to teachers: The problem may need to be rephrased to require students either to show all their work or to use the data in the table to make the estimates for parts b, c, and d. (See student C's work.)

Solution

a. $\dfrac{34}{80} \times 2100 = 892.5$ Either 892 or 893

b. Dependent

   If A is the event that a student plays a musical instrument and B is the event that a student plays sports, then

$$P(B) = \dfrac{46}{80} \text{ and } P(B|A) = \dfrac{14}{34}.$$

   Since $P(B) \neq P(B|A)$, they are dependent events.

c. $\dfrac{14}{80} = \dfrac{7}{40} = .175$

d. $\dfrac{14}{46} = \dfrac{7}{23} \approx .304$

Student Work

Student A

Student A answered part a correctly. In part b this student used an incorrect ratio to determine $P(A|B)$ but shows an understanding of how to determine whether an event is independent. His work indicates a misunderstanding of how to read the table to determine probability for an event. He also simplified his ratio erroneously and used this incorrect answer in part c. He also simplified his ratio incorrectly in part d. His arithmetic errors may be a result of carelessness, or they may indicate a weakness in working with rational numbers.

a. $^{34}/_{80} = \frac{17}{40}$ $\frac{17}{40} = \frac{x}{2100}$ 893 students

b. $P(A) = ^{17}/_{40}$
   $P(A|B) = ^{14}/_{80} = ^{7}/_{40}$ $\frac{17}{40} \neq ^{7}/_{40}$ dependent

c. $P(A \text{ and } B) = \frac{17}{40} \cdot \frac{7}{40} = \frac{119}{1600}$

d. $P(A|B) = \frac{14}{46} = ^{7}/_{24}$

Student B

Student B answered parts a and c correctly but seems to have held a misconception about how to test for independent events. The student also demonstrated a misunderstanding or misconception about how to answer part d. The work indicates that the student is competent in working with rational numbers.

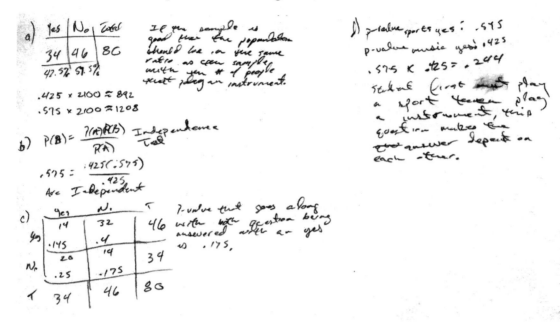

Student C

Although student C answered part a incorrectly, he explained the correct procedure for answering the question and interpreting the table. On parts b, c, and d he simply answered the questions on the basis of his personal experience or through observations of high school students participating in sports and music rather than on his knowledge of probability.

a. I would expect 392.5 to play an instrument. Because out of the eighty kids 34 play instruments or .425. So you multiply .425 by 2100 students.

b. No, because if you play football you cannot be in the band.

c. I estimate the probability to be less than 25% because the chance of a student being able to play music and sports are rare.

d. I estimate the probability to be around 35% because a large amount of students play sports and a medium amount of students play an instrument.

Standard: Understand and apply basic concepts of probability

Expectation: Understand the concepts of conditional probability and independent events; understand how to compute the probability of a compound event

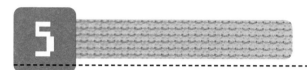

Twenty-five people watched a movie showing at Empire Theaters. Of them, fifteen order a drink, eight order popcorn, and seven order candy. Two people order all three items, three order drink and candy, five order drink and popcorn, and three order popcorn and candy.

a. Display the results in a Venn diagram.
b. What is the probability that a moviegoer who buys a drink will also buy popcorn?

> **About the mathematics:** The Venn diagram makes setting up the probability for each event easier for the problem posed. The solution does not involve just an algebraic computation of a formula.
> **Solution:** See page 142.

Solution

a.

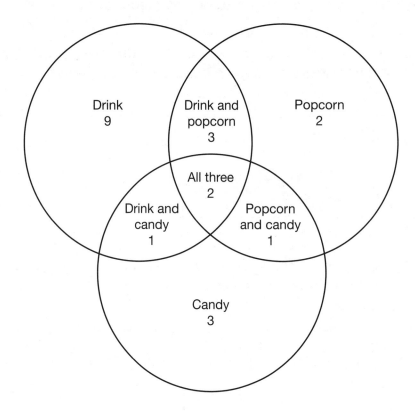

b. $^5/_{15}$, or $^1/_3$

Standard: Select and use appropriate statistical methods to analyze data

Expectations: For bivariate measurement data, be able to display a scatter-plot, describe its shape, and determine regression coefficients, regression equations, and correlation coefficients using technological tools; identify trends in bivariate data and find functions that model the data or transform the data so that they can be modeled

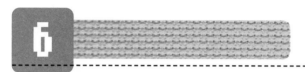

The following data set compares the average number of hours studied per week with a student's GPA.

Hours studied	12	8	2	6	10	5	10	9	3	4
GPA	3.97	3.20	2.15	2.95	3.45	2.86	3.75	3.05	2.45	2.20

a. Graph the data, and find a line of best fit.
b. Add a point that would not change the slope of the line of best fit but would increase the *y*-intercept when *y* represents the GPA and *x* represents "hours studied."
c. Add a point that would increase the slope of the line of best fit.

About the mathematics: This problem is a typical textbook problem that has been enhanced by parts b and c, which require the student to consider what variables affect the outcome. With the use of a graphing calculator, several solutions are possible.

Solution

a. Use technology to calculate the linear regression $\hat{y} = 1.74x + 1.8$.

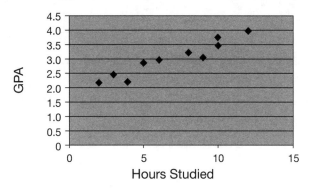

b. A point must be inserted in the middle of the data set and above the data that are present. An example would be the point (7, 3.5).

c. A point must be inserted at the far left and below the data set, indicating a low number of hours studied paired with a low GPA, or at the far right and above the data set, indicating a high number of hours studied paired with a high GPA. Examples would be the point (2, 1.0) and the point (10, 4.0).

Standard: Select and use appropriate statistical methods to analyze data

Expectation: For univariate measurement data, be able to display the distribution, describe its shape, and select and calculate summary statistics

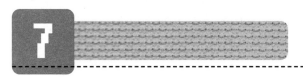

A class of 350 graduating seniors found their heights to be approximately normally distributed, with a mean of 68 inches and a standard deviation of 3 inches.

a. Draw the normal distribution, labeling the mean and ±3 standard deviations from the mean.

b. How many students' heights lie between 1 and 2 standard deviations above the mean? How do you know?

c. How many students' heights fall less than 2 standard deviations below the mean? How do you know?

About the mathematics: This item allows the student to be able to display the distribution, describe its shape, and select and calculate summary statistics. The problem also has the student generate the standard bell curve and evaluate its meaning in the context of the problem posed.

Solution

a.

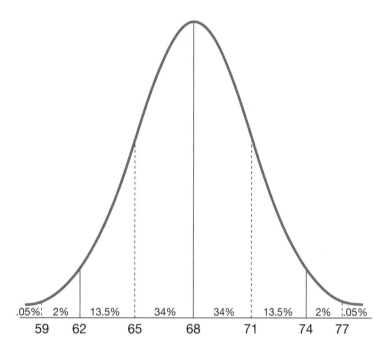

	.05%	2%	13.5%	34%	34%	13.5%	2%	.05%
	59	62	65	68	71	74	77	

b. Because these values are normally distributed, 13.5% of the 350 students, or approximately 47 students, have heights that lie between 1 and 2 standard deviations above the mean.

c. For the same reason, 2.5% of the 350 students, or approximately 8 or 9 students, have heights that fall less than 2 standard deviations below the mean.

Standard: Select and use appropriate statistical methods to analyze data

Expectation: For univariate measurement data, be able to display the distribution, describe its shape, and select and calculate summary statistics

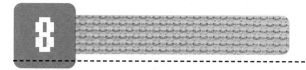

The following data set is a list of scores on Mrs. Davis's third-period geometry test: 20, 56, 96, 84, 84, 83, 91, 70, 74, 88, 64, 67, 63, 84, 88, 84, 70, 73, 75, 71, 84, 90, 85, 87, 84.

a. Draw a box-and-whiskers plot of the data.
b. Describe the center, shape, and spread.
c. If Mrs. Davis were to discuss the results with her class, what important observations might she make about the data?

About the mathematics: This item allows students to display the distribution, describe its shape, and calculate summary statistics. The problem also allows students to generate an appropriate graph and display an understanding of the data.

Solution

a.

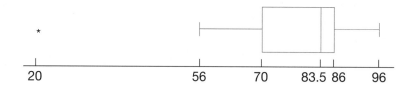

b. The center of the distribution is in the upper 70s, the shape is skewed left, and the spread shows that the scores are grouped tightly except for the score of 20.

c. Mrs. Davis would discuss the facts that the score of 20 is an outlier and that by removing the score, the mean score in the class would increase while the standard deviation would decrease. She would point out that removing the score of 20 has little effect on the five-number summary. This outcome shows that mean and standard deviation are nonresistant, whereas the five-number summary consists of resistant measures. When the score of 20 is removed, the shape goes from being skewed left to being approximately normal.

Standard: Understand and apply basic concepts of probability

Expectation: Understand the concepts of sample space and probability distribution and construct sample spaces and distributions in simple cases

Challenger

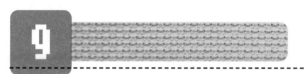

What is the geometric probability that two positive numbers, x and y (both less than 1), written down at random, together with the number 1, yield a trio of numbers $(x, y, 1)$ that are the sides of an obtuse-angled triangle?

Source: Adapted from *Ingenuity in Mathematics* (Honsberger 1970, p. 4)
About the mathematics: This problem is challenging yet accessible for students with an algebra and trigonometry background, although the teacher may need to present it with hints or use guided instruction.
Note to teacher: This problem is crossed referenced with Geometry. See page 107 for the solution.

6

Professional Development

EVERY assessment is an attempt to gather information about what students know and are able to do. The assessment itself, whether it is a test or a posed question, is just the beginning of the assessment process. The evidence of a student's thinking revealed in the student's response must be interpreted, and an inference must be made about the level of understanding reflected in that response. Effective classroom assessment allows a teacher to identify individual differences among students in a class (Bright and Joyner 2004).

Providing meaningful feedback to students is an integral step in the assessment process. If students are to learn from teacher feedback, it must specifically address errors and strategies and must include suggestions on how to improve. Feedback that is too general or that focuses on superficial learning of procedures rather than on deep understanding does not help students learn (Wilson and Kenney 2003). Feedback should be designed to help students grow in confidence and ability in evaluating their own mathematical progress and performance.

This chapter focuses on two important aspects of professional development for preservice and in-service teachers that are central to assessment: (1) analysis of student errors and (2) scoring and rubrics.

Error Analysis

A helpful approach to understanding the significance of students' errors is to think about those errors as being either conceptual or procedural. Conceptual understanding may be thought of as understanding the "big idea," so we, as teachers, should look at students' work to determine whether it shows evidence to support this understanding. This component of assessing student work is challenging because the way in which students present their thinking may or may not indicate their conceptual understanding. Conceptual understanding can be thought of as the substance of an idea, and it can be distinguished from the way in which students communicate their thinking, which can be thought of as the presentation of an idea. Both substantive and presentation errors are, of course, possible in work that addresses either procedural or conceptual ideas (Bright and Joyner 2003).

In examining the student work in this chapter, we have tried to understand whether the student errors indicate conceptual misunderstanding; are procedural errors; or, because of faulty presentation, miscommunicate conceptual understanding.

Number and Operations

Sample 1

List these numbers in increasing order: $2^{800}, 3^{600}, 5^{400}, 6^{200}$

Smallest 6^{200}

Second 5^{400}

Third 3^{600}

Largest 2^{800}

How did you decide?

Though the base number is larger, the true value is based on the exponents, so the largest value of exponent will be the largest number.

Sample 2

List these numbers in increasing order: $2^{800}, 3^{600}, 5^{400}, 6^{200}$

Smallest _____ 3^{600}

Second _____ 5^{400}

Third _____ 3^{600}

Largest _____ 2^{800}

How did you decide?

It just seemed like the most logical way to arrange them without finding out actual values, because even if the base is small, a larger exponent will cause the figure to grow substantially.

Error: Students appear to have assumed that the largest exponent will produce the largest number. This assumption suggests a conceptual misunderstanding.

Comments: These students should be encouraged to investigate smaller numbers and observe patterns to help them understand the error. For example, the teacher might suggest that the students first predict the larger value, then compare 6^2 and 2^4 in expanded form. Next the teacher might ask the students to predict and compare other pairs, including pairs with the same bases and pairs with different bases and the same exponents, for example, 3^4 and 3^6, 3^4 and 6^4. This common error could possibly come from transposing the meaning of the exponent and that of the base. The use of a calculator would be appropriate in this teaching setting because the focus is conceptual and not computational.

Sample 3

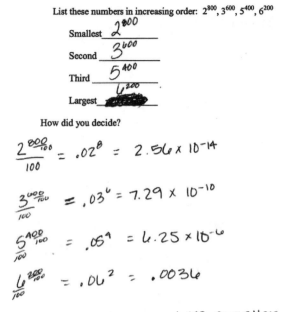

List these numbers in increasing order: $2^{800}, 3^{600}, 5^{400}, 6^{200}$

Smallest 2^{800}

Second 3^{600}

Third 5^{400}

Largest ~~6^{200}~~.

How did you decide?

$$\frac{2^{\frac{800}{100}}}{100} = .02^8 = 2.56 \times 10^{-14}$$

$$\frac{3^{\frac{600}{100}}}{100} = .03^6 = 7.29 \times 10^{-10}$$

$$\frac{5^{\frac{400}{100}}}{100} = .05^4 = 6.25 \times 10^{-6}$$

$$\frac{6^{\frac{200}{100}}}{100} = .06^2 = .0036$$

I made each number smaller & easier to compute by dividing both numbers by 100. I was able to put these numbers in the calculator and I got answers that I could measure.

Error: This student appears to have incorrectly applied the order of operations. Although this response may suggest a procedural error, it also strongly indicates that the student has communicated a misconception regarding the application of the order of operations when dealing with exponents.

Comments: The student appears to have used a problem-solving technique typically known as "solve a simpler but similar problem, find a pattern, and apply that pattern in solving the original problem." The student may also have applied an operational technique used in solving equations and expressed by students as "what you do to one side of an equation, you do to the other." In this example, the student has divided both the base and the exponent by the same number. The student may have also misapplied the power-to-a-power rule and multiplied both the base and the exponent by $1/100$. In either instance, the student could be given smaller values, such as 4, and asked to write it in exponential form, 2^2, then apply his technique to the simpler problem. When the student would then divide the exponent and the base by the same number, in this example, 2, to check the accuracy of his technique, he would find that his process would result in 1^1, or 1, and would realize that 1 does not equal 4.

Sample 4

What is the units digit of 3^{1992}? Write a convincing mathematical argument that supports your solution.

$3^1 = 3$

$3^2 = 9$

$3^3 = 27$

$3^4 = 81$

$3^5 = 243$

$3^6 = 729$

$3^7 = 2187$

$3^8 = 6561$

$3^9 = 19683$

$3^{10} = 59049$

$3^{11} = 177147$

$3^{12} = 531441$

$3^{13} = 1594323$

$3^{14} = 4782969$

$3^{15} = 14348907$

$3^{16} = 43046721$

$3^{1992} = ?$

When 3 is multiplied exponentially by units of 4, the units digit is always one: $3^4 = 81$ $3^8 = 6561$ $3^{16} = 43046721$

4 is a factor of 1992, thus the units digit of 3^{1992} is one.

Error: The error here is in the presentation of the student's thinking. The student used a patterning technique to solve the problem. Her thinking is evident in the presentation of the mathematics; however, the wording to support that thinking is awkward and not mathematically precise.

Comments: Additional practice and work would help the student grow in her ability to communicate mathematically. The writing process in mathematics, as well as in English, involves a cycle of revision. Many teachers encourage students to form peer pairs for reading and revising their written work in mathematics.

Sample 5

Given the expression $1! + 2! + \ldots + 205!$, what is the units digit of the sum? Clearly communicate your reasoning and explain how you know that your response is mathematically correct.

$1! = 1$
$2! = 2$
$3! = 6$
$4! = 24$
$5! = 120$
$6! = 720$

$2! + 2! = 3 + 3! = 9 + 4! = 33 + 5! = 153 + 6! = 873 + 7! = 5913$

$5913 + 8! = 46233 + 9! = 409113 + 10! = 4037913 + 11! = 1395913$

$1! + 2! + 3! + 4!$

$5! =$ units of 0

Therefore, any $n!$ after that will have a unit digits of 0. And because we are adding factorials to each other, and the unit digits is 0, the units digit will stay the same for every $n! \geq 5$. Because $1! + 2! \ldots n! =$ a units digit of 3, and because any factorial greater than that has a units digit of 0, $1! + 2! + \ldots 205!$ will have a units digit of 3

Error: This work contains evidence of a conceptual understanding of factorials. The student's solution of 3 is correct, but his explanation contains incorrect mathematical notation. The presentation of the student's thinking contains the most common error found in students' work. That error is illustrated in the first line of the solution, where the student writes

$$1! + 2! = 3 + 3! = 9 + 4! = 33 + 5! = 153 + 6! = 873 + 7! = 5913.$$

This inappropriate chain of equalities may illustrate a basic error in the conceptual understanding of the equality symbol.

Comments: This student expresses his solution process as a chain of equalities. It may also be that the student understands the equality symbol as more than "the answer goes here" and has used the symbol to replace "and then." Whatever the source of his misunderstanding, the student requires additional feedback on his written communication, and, as in the previous example, may benefit from working in peer pairs prior to turning in written work.

Sample 6

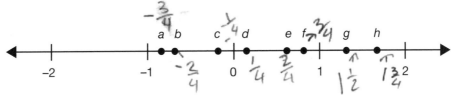

Given the points with coordinates $a, b, c, \ldots, h$ as shown, which point is closest to—

a. ab?

b. $|c|$?

c. $\dfrac{1}{f}$?

d. $\sqrt{e}$?

e. $\sqrt{h}$?

Error: This student work displays evidence of a misunderstanding of the concept as well as procedural errors that may or may not be the result of carelessness. In trying to answer the question, this student substituted inappropriate values. The values selected reveal that this student has deficits in working with and understanding rational numbers. His attempt to solve the problem relies on the use of specific values rather than on the more abstract relationships. This student's approach of using approximate values did not serve him well, not only because his choices were only multiples of $^1/_4$ but also because he did not pay attention to the intervals between the points on the number line. The work from part (a) indicates that his answer would have been "f," which is incorrect. This error may or may not have been a careless mistake in simplifying fractions.

Comments: Students should be given many opportunities to work with situations that can be resolved with or without substituting approximate values. If they do substitute values, they need experiences that will empower them to analyze their answers with many different values to be sure that they are not drawing incorrect conclusions. Teachers could then discuss the advantages of using properties of numbers rather than specific values to generalize answers. Certainly, this student should be interviewed so that the teacher can better understand his thinking and guide him to a better understanding of the concepts addressed in this problem.

Algebra

Assessment Item

If $xy = 1$ and x is greater than 0, which of the following statements is true? Show the work that justifies your answer.

a. When x is greater than 1, y is negative.
b. When x is greater than 1, y is greater than 1.
c. When x is less than 1, y is less than 1.
d. As x increases, y increases.
e. As x increases, y decreases.

Sample 1

$$xy = 1$$

a. $2(-1) = -1 \quad xy \neq 1 \quad \text{False}$

b. $2(2) = 4 \quad xy \neq 1 \quad \text{false}$

c. $.9(.9) = .81$
$.5(.5) = .25 \quad xy \neq 1 \quad \text{false}$

d. $(1)1 = 1$
$2(2) = 4 \quad \text{false}$
$3(3) = 9$

e. $1(1) = 1.$
$2(\frac{1}{2}) = 1$
$3(\frac{1}{3}) = 1 \quad \text{True}$
$4(\frac{1}{4}) = 1$

E is the only true statement.

Sample 2

If $xy = 1$ and x is greater than 0, which of the following statements is true?

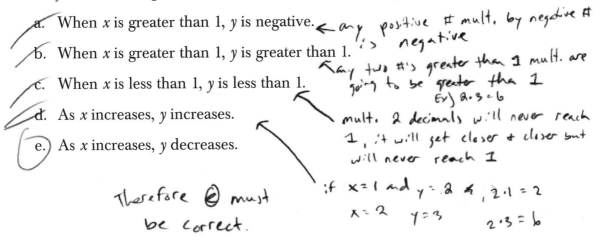

a. When x is greater than 1, y is negative. ← any positive # mult. by negative # is negative

b. When x is greater than 1, y is greater than 1. ← any two #'s greater than 1 mult. are going to be greater than 1
Ex) 2·3 = 6

c. When x is less than 1, y is less than 1. ← mult. 2 decimals will never reach 1, it will get closer & closer but will never reach 1

d. As x increases, y increases.

e. As x increases, y decreases.

Therefore ⓔ must be correct.

if $x = 1$ and $y = .2$ & , $2·1 = 2$
$x = 2$ $y = 3$ $2·3 = 6$

Error: Although both of these students use a valuable technique of finding counterexamples to eliminate answers and both answer the question correctly, they may be communicating a misunderstanding. They both appear to be operating under the misconception that when substituted values happen to make a statement true, the statement is always true.

Comments: An interview with the students would clarify the level to which the students understand the limitation of substituting in only values that make the statements true. Both of these students should be encouraged to solve the equation for y and generate a graph and table of values. The next step would be to use the graph and table to determine whether the statements are true. This approach would help students visualize the validity of the statements. They could then use the graph to articulate their conclusion. This problem, along with the problem that follows it, should be taken together as examples of illustrating students' understanding of functions through graphs and equations.

Many extensions of this problem are possible, for example: Sketch a graph with no real roots or with one real root. What must be true about a, b, and c if the graph of the function $y = ax^2 + bx + c$ lies in only three quadrants? Students can use trial and error with their calculators. Both of these problems are calculator-rich and offer an effective use of technology.

Sample 3

4. The price of a particular product doubles every 35 years. If the price of the product was $16.50 on January 1, 1996, then the price of the product will be $36.50 in the year
a. 2028
b. 2031

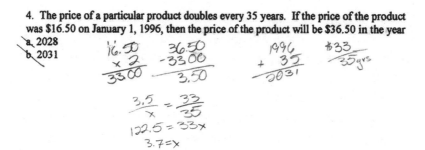

Error: This solution contains procedural errors as well computational errors. Although this student answered the question correctly (not shown), the work does not indicate an understanding of how to do the problem.

Comments: This response is a good example of why looking beyond the correct answer is necessary. The student determined that in the year 2031, the price of the product would be double the price of the product in 1996. She then doubled $36.50. (Notice the arithmetic error of 73.1.) The student's strategy is unclear. This student needs to be interviewed so that she can explain her approach to the problem.

Sample 4

4. The price of a particular product doubles every 35 years. If the price of the product was $16.50 on January 1, 1996, then the price of the product will be $36.50 in the year
a. 2028
b. 2031

Error: This response appears to communicate a misunderstanding on the part of the student about when it is appropriate to use a proportion to solve a problem.

Comments: Although this student chose the correct answer, her work does not support an understanding of the concept. She appears to have reasoned that if the price took 35 years to increase to $33, then the additional increase of $3.50 would take 3.7 years. She then added 3.7 (rounded to 4) to 2031 to get 2035. Since 2035 was not one of the choices, she chose the closest answer, 2036 (not shown). An interview with this student might be helpful to guide her thinking about why using a proportion is not an appropriate strategy for this problem.

Assessment Item

In February 2000 the cost of sending a letter by first-class mail was 33 cents for the first ounce and an additional 22 cents for each additional ounce or portion thereof through 13 ounces. Choose the graph that best represents the cost of mailing a letter that weighs 4 ounces or less. (See chapter 2, problem 3, for the complete item.)

Sample 5

> Graph (a) cannot express this relationship - as you cannot have a negative weight, as seen in the graph. Likewise graph (d) cannot be correct since it isn't a function, so if you had 2 ounces, would you pay 55 or 77 cents? So the answer must be either (b) or (c). My guess is C, since it has an open circle on the y-axis, meaning if you had a zero weight package, you'd pay nothing. As graph (b) suggests, if you weren't sending anything at all, why would you have to pay? C is the most logical, as you get to the first ounce, you pay 33¢, then immediately after you rise up to the second "stairstep."

Error: Why this student states that graph (a) contains a negative weight is not clear. His reasoning for the other distractors is logical.

Sample 6

In February 2000 the cost of sending a letter by first-class mail was 33 cents for the first ounce and an additional 22 cents for each additional ounce or portion thereof through 13 ounces. Choose the graph that best represents the cost of mailing a letter that weighs 4 ounces or less. (See chapter 2, problem 3, for the complete item.)

$1 \rightarrow \$.33$

$2 \rightarrow \$.55$

the correct
graph is b
because a letter costs
33¢ even if it weighs
under an ounce
2 ounces cost $55
So closed circles
must be on
first part of
higher amount

Error: This student provides evidence of understanding the pricing of a stamp on the basis of its weight; however he does not interpret the meaning of the graph at (0, 0.33). With some prodding questions, he may very well be able to identify his error.

Comments: Students in general had difficulty with the open-closed concept for the graph, and many were not able to interpret it correctly. This inability to interpret step graphs may be due to lack of experience with them. Students may just need opportunities to discuss the meaning of endpoints when used in a step function. This discussion could lead to questions about range and domain for graphs of this type.

Other problems could be generated from this item. For example, students could be given the data only and be asked to find a function that describes the data. In doing so, they might generate a linear function with a constant rate of change of 22 cents per ounce. But students need to understand that the graph that describes the data is a step function and is the only function that makes sense in the context of the given problem.

Geometry

Assessment Item

The vertices of the triangle PQR are the points $P(1, 2)$, $Q(4, 6)$, and $R(-4, 12)$. Which one of the following statements about triangle PQR must be true?

a. PQR is a right triangle with the right angle at P.
b. PQR is a right triangle with the right angle at Q.
c. PQR is a right triangle with the right angle at R.
d. PQR is not a right triangle.

Justify your answer.

Sample 1

a. PQR is a right triangle with the right angle at P.
b. PQR is a right triangle with the right angle at Q.
c. PQR is a right triangle with the right angle at R.
d. PQR is not a right triangle.

Justify your answer.

none of them line up correctly

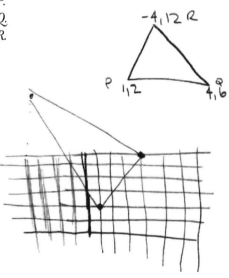

Error: This response seems to indicate a misunderstanding of how to appropriately support a mathematical argument. The student based her answer on her own drawing, which is not drawn to scale, and neglected to do any mathematics to support her claim.

Comments: Teachers should emphasize that drawings are not always drawn to scale and should not influence students' answers unless they back their conclusions with the appropriate mathematics. With graphing calculators we look at mathematics more visually than ever before in our classrooms, so the "reminder" to support conclusions with appropriate mathematics becomes increasingly more important.

Assessment Item

The rectangular coordinates of three points in a plane are $Q(-3, -1)$, $R(-2, 3)$, and $S(1, -3)$. A fourth point T is chosen so that vector ST is equal to twice vector QR. The y-coordinate of T is _____.

a. -11
b. -7
c. -1
d. 1
e. 5

Show how you got your answer.

Sample 2

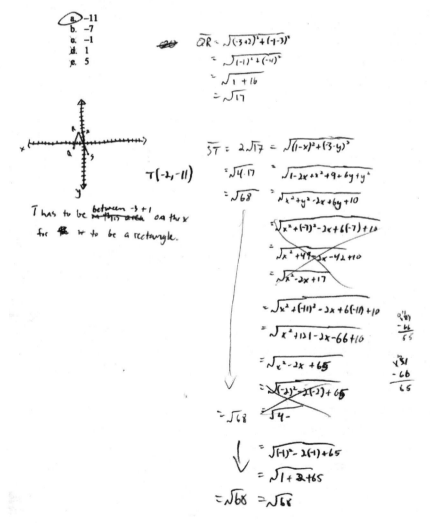

Error: This student's work provides evidence of a procedural understanding of how to find the magnitude of a vector. It also shows that the student knew that the length of the vector must be twice the length of the original one. What is not evident is whether the student would be able to begin to solve the problem if it were a short-answer question and thus did not contain distractors with which to use a guess-and-check strategy.

Comments: Without the multiple-choice answers in this problem, the student might not have made this attempt, and an instructor could easily miss the concepts the student does know. He had no problems setting up the situation correctly. His difficulty appears to be the fact that two variables but only one equation were involved. By substituting the various possible answers for y into the equation, he eliminated a variable to obtain one equation with one unknown. But he did not attempt to solve for x except in the instance in which he used $y = -11$. He realized that -1 for x would give him a vector with a correct magnitude. This vector, however, was vector TS, not vector ST as instructed. A discussion with this student about his procedure would probably yield some very interesting insight into his reasoning and possibly provide the student with information that would clarify his misunderstandings.

Assessment Item

In triangle *ABC* below, the altitudes *BN* and *CM* intersect at point *S*. The measure of angle *MSB* is 40°, and the measure of angle *SBC* is 20°. Write a *proof* of the following statement: "Triangle *ABC* is isosceles." (See chapter 3, problem 6, for the complete item.)

Sample 3

1) $\overline{BN}$ and $\overline{CM}$ are altitudes of △ABC; $m\angle MSB=40°$, $m\angle NBC=20°$	1) Given
2) ∠BMC and ∠CNB are right angles	2) definition of altitude
3) $m\angle BMC=90°$; $m\angle CNB=90°$	3) definition of a right angle
4) ∠MSB and ∠NSC are vertical angles	4) definition of vertical angles
5) $m\angle MSB=m\angle NSC$	5) vertical angles are congruent
6) $m\angle NSC=40°$	6) substitution
7) $m\angle MBN+m\angle BMC+m\angle MSB=180°$ $m\angle NCM+m\angle CNB+m\angle NSC=180°$	7) the sum of the angles in a triangle equals 180°
8) $m\angle MBN+90°+40°=180°$ $m\angle NCB+90°+40°=180°$	8) substitution
9) $m\angle MBN+130°=180°$ $m\angle NCB+130°=180°$	9) substitution
10) $m\angle MBN=50°$ $m\angle NCB=50°$	10) subtraction property of (=)
11) ∠MSB and ∠BSC make a linear pair	11) definition of a linear pair
12) $m\angle MSB+m\angle BSC=180°$	12) the sum of ∠'s in a linear pair =180°
13) $40°+m\angle BSC=180°$	13) substitution
14) $m\angle BSC=140°$	14) subtraction property of equality
15) $m\angle SBC+m\angle BSC+m\angle SCB=180°$	15) the sum of ∠'s in a △=180°
16) $20°+140°+m\angle SCB=180°$	16) substitution
17) $m\angle SCB=20°$	17) subtraction property of (=)
18) $m\angle ABC=m\angle ABN+m\angle NBC$ $m\angle ACB=m\angle ACM+m\angle MCB$	18) Angle Addition Postulate
19) $m\angle ABC=50°+20°$ $m\angle ACB=20°+50°$	19) substitution
20) $m\angle ABC=70°$ $m\angle ACB=70°$	20) substitution
21) $m\angle ABC=m\angle ACB$	21) Transitive property of (=)
22) △ABC is isosceles	22) If 2 angles of a △ are congruent, then the △ is isosceles.

Error: Although this proof reveals several minor errors and omissions, it does indicate that the student understands both the concept and procedure of how to prove that a triangle is isosceles. One of the minor errors occurs in statement 2, which should have stated as the reason the fact that the segments are perpendicular. Then the student could have made the statement about right angles and used the reason that perpendicular lines form right angles. He also states that two angles have the same measure (in statement 5), whereas he should have said that they are congruent first, using the correct reason that vertical angles are congruent. His next statement could then have stated their equal measure. A statement is needed between steps 11 and 12 that indicates that the two angles are supplementary because angles that form a linear pair are supplementary. The reason for statement 12 would then be "Definition of supplementary." Statements are needed between steps 21 and 22, one to indicate that the angles are congruent and another to state that the sides are congruent. Once the opposite sides are established as being congruent, then the student can write that the triangle is isosceles because of the definition of isosceles.

Comments: Students need to be able to support their work with mathematical proofs. The proofs may take the form of a paragraph or the more traditional two-column proof. Either way, students must include accurate mathematical arguments.

Sample 4

Angle MSB is 40° so opposite angles are congruent, making NSC 40° also. If angle N ◦ angle M are both 90° and we know that all complete triangles add up to 180°. So if 2 of the 3 angles equals 130° then the final angles of ⒝ NSC ◦ MSB is is 50°. Add 50° to the other 20° given for angle B (which is also the same for angle C) b/c the angle measurement for MSB ◦ NSC are all congruent, we know the full measurement of angle C ◦ B i's 70%. In an Isosceles triangle, 2 sides must be equal length ◦ in order for them to be equal in length, 2 of the 3 angles must also be congruent. So, since ∠B ◦ ∠C are both 70°, then the triangle ABC is isosceles.

Sample 5

$\triangle BNC$ is a right $\triangle$ and $\angle B = 20°$ $\therefore$ $\angle C = 70°$

Since $\triangle SMB$ is a right triangle, $\angle SBM = 50°$

$\angle SBC + \angle SBM = \angle B$ $\therefore$ $20° + 50° = 70°$

Rule of an Isosceles triangle is that the two base angles are congruent. $\angle B \cong \angle C$.

Error: Samples 4 and 5 use a paragraph format to make their mathematical arguments. These students appear not to know what needs to be included to make a substantive proof. This deficiency may be due to lack of experience.
Comments: These two students (samples 4 and 5) were the only ones who attempted paragraph proofs. Their proofs are missing some of the major elements necessary to create a convincing mathematical argument. Since few axioms or theorems are referenced, the arguments are less than robust and complete.

General Comments on the Proof Problems

After pilot testing the proof problem in several school districts in different parts of the country, we found that no student could produce what we considered to be a "perfect" proof. The proofs either lacked essential statements or contained incorrect reasons. Teachers can help students produce successful proofs by devising fill-in-the-missing statement (or missing-reason) activities. Students should also be encouraged to think through a problem and write down all the theorems, definitions, and postulates that they would use in a proof, whereby teachers can then help them organize their thinking. For this particular problem, most students evidently understood the definition of isosceles triangle and what they would need to show for the triangles to be isosceles. The students just could not structure their mathematical arguments in a logical, carefully reasoned proof.

Assessment Item

Two marbles are sitting side by side in a glass container. The base of the container is 10 units in length, and the radius of the smaller marble is 2 units.

a. Describe a strategy that you could use to find the radius of the large marble.
b. Use this strategy to calculate the radius of the large marble.

Sample 6

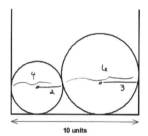

a. Describe a strategy that you could use to find the radius of the large marble.

Double the radius of the smaller marble to get 4 units. Subtract 4 from the base length to get 6 units for the big marble. Divide 6 by 2 to get the big marbles radius, 3 units.

b. Use this strategy to calculate the radius of the large marble.

3 units

Error: This work appears to indicate a conceptual misunderstanding. This student did not analyze the problem correctly; he or she used the incorrect technique of assuming that the radii lie on a line parallel to the base.

Comments: At a first glance at this problem, many students would make this same error. To help students see that the marbles "overlap" a bit, a teacher may want to bring in marbles of two different sizes and allow the students to place them on the same base. Students could then check the total length if the marbles were placed side by side. In a problem like this, with such a high level of complexity, students should be given opportunity to model the problem. A guided discussion that would allow students to comment on the difficult aspects of the problem would be beneficial so that all students would be aware of the difficulties and take them into account when solving the problem. This problem could be used as a challenge problem, a performance assessment, or a group project in which students present their solutions to the class, depending on the ability level of the students.

Measurement

Assessment Item

Use the grid below to answer the questions. Show as much of your work as possible. Sketch a smaller square inside the given square so that the smaller square is half the area of the larger square. Write an explanation to convince another person that your new, smaller square is truly half the area of the original square.

Sample 1

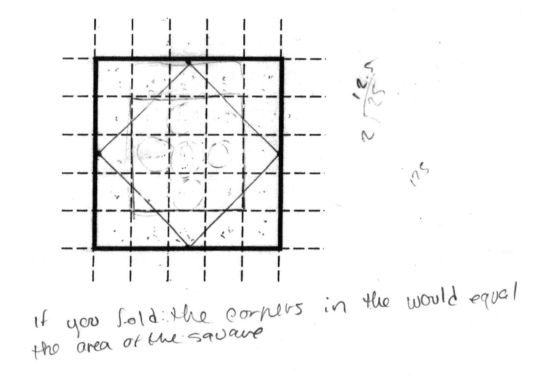

If you fold the corners in the would equal the area of the square

Error: Although this student seems to understand how to go about solving the problem, not enough work is shown, nor sufficient justification given for the work, to know whether the student can make a convincing argument that his square is truly half the area of the original square.

Comments: Although no justification is included, this approach could be modeled by having students cut out a square, mark off the midpoints, and fold in the corners. Other students could then be called on to use mathematics to verify this student's conjecture and to justify that the figure is a square and not a rhombus.

Sample 2

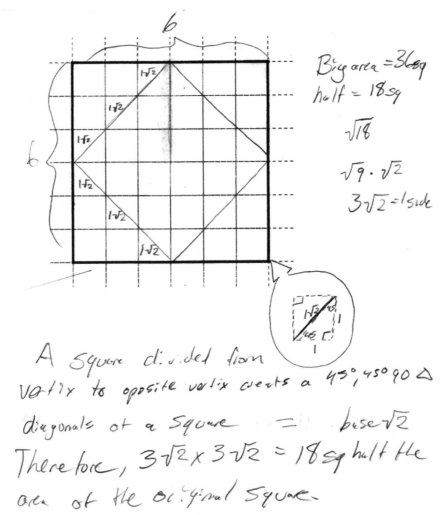

Big area = 36 sq

half = 18 sq

$\sqrt{18}$

$\sqrt{9} \cdot \sqrt{2}$

$3\sqrt{2} = 1$ side

A square divided from vertix to opposite vertix creates a 45°, 45° 90 △ diagonals of a square = base √2

Therefore, $3\sqrt{2} \times 3\sqrt{2} = 18$ sq half the area of the original square.

Comments: This student used a solid mathematical approach to verify his drawing.

Sample 3

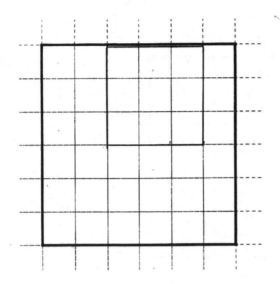

$$A = \tfrac{1}{2} A'$$
$$A = \tfrac{1}{2} \overset{18}{\cancel{36}}_{1}$$
$$A \neq 18$$
$$A = 9$$

doesn't work because to get 18 it wouldn't be a square anymore.

Error: This student's work reveals a conceptual misunderstanding of how to divide a square so that the resulting area is one-half the original. It also indicates a conceptual misunderstanding of irrational numbers. The procedural evidence does support the student's understanding of how to find the area of a rectangle.

Comments: This student sketched a 3 × 3 square but then determined that it would not work, because 18 is not a perfect square number. The student needs to review and understand the concept of irrational numbers and how they can represent the sides of squares. This student would benefit from experiences in modeling problems like this using paper models or geoboard models.

Sample 4

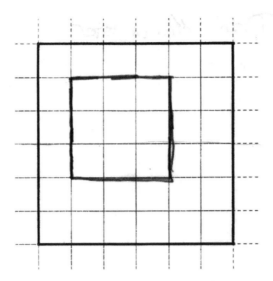

The larger square has a side length of 6 squares. If you divide 6 by 2 you get 3 making the other sides of the square, that is ½ the size of the large square, 3.

Error: This solution demonstrates a conceptual misunderstanding about the relationship between the scale factors for length and area. The student appears to think that both the length and the area are linear measures.

Comments: This student uses the same approach as the student whose work is given on the previous page, but she believes that she can create a new square with half the area of the original square. A teacher could have the student count the squares in the new figure to determine that it does not have half the area of the larger. This error is the same as the one in chapter 4, "Measurement," in that it represents the common error that students make by assuming that doubling (or halving) a side of a square will double (or halve) the area.

Comments on student work on the grid problem
No student included a justification that the new figure has four right angles and is indeed a square.

Data Analysis

Assessment Item

A warning system installation consists of two independent alarms having probabilities of operating in an emergency of 0.95 and 0.90, respectively. Find the probability that at least one alarm operates in an emergency. Show your work. (See chapter 5, problem 1, for the complete item.)

Sample 1

      a. 0.995
      b. 0.975
      c. 0.95
      d. 0.90
      (e) 0.855

$$P(A) = \text{Alarm 1 works}$$

$$P(B) = \text{Alarm 2 works}$$

$$P(A \cup B) = .95 \cdot .90 = .855$$

Error: This error appears to be a conceptual misunderstanding between the meaning of an "and" situation versus that of an "or" situation, in that the student applied the incorrect probability rule.

Comments: Some students have difficulty distinguishing between the sense of *and* and that of *or* in probability problems when the statement does not use those exact words. *At least* is a common phrase in probability, and students often make the same mistake this student made. If a student can reason that *at least* means that either alarm A works or alarm B works, or that they both work, the student can usually solve the problem successfully. However, if a student does not reason this way, he or she often thinks of the statement as meaning that both alarms work simultaneously, as this student did. This misconception may be an example of what can happen when students simply memorize rules and do not fully understand the meaning of what they have memorized.

Assessment Item

If the population increases by the same average rate from the year 1990 to the year 2005 as in the years from 1975 to 1985, approximately what is the expected population by the year 2005? Justify your answer. (See chapter 5, problem 2, for the complete item.)

Sample 2

a. 47 million
b. 50 million
c. 53 million
d. 58 million

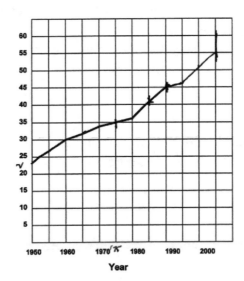

'75-'85=6 mil.
'90-'05=6 mil

45+6=51

'75-'80 = ≠ 10 million

5 years ≠ +10 mil

55

'75 → '85 = 10 years = + 6 mil

'90 → 2005 = 15 yr = + 6 mil

45 mil + 6 mil = 51 mil → closer to 50 mil.

Error: Whether this error is procedural or conceptual is difficult to discern. The student either misread the problem or did not account for the difference in the lengths of the time intervals.

Comments: The student correctly finds the average rate of increase from 1975 to 1985 as 6 million people in 10 years. She also realizes that the second interval from 1990 to 2005 was 15 years, not 10 years as in the previous interval. However, at this point the student simply adds the 45 million people in 1990 to the 6 million to arrive at an answer of 51 million, which is closest to the choice of 50 million and leads to her choice of b as her answer. This answer would be correct if the increase over the 15-year interval was the same as the increase over the 10-year interval. The words *average rate* tell us that the increase in the 15-year interval should be 9 million, not 6 million, giving an answer of 54 million; thus the answer of 53 million, choice c, is closest. Whether the student has misread the problem or has simply missed the change in interval length is difficult to determine. An interview with the student would let us know where her error occurred.

Assessment Item

The diagram below shows the results of a two-question survey administered to 80 randomly selected students at Highcrest High School.

Do you play on a sports team?

	Yes	No
No	32	14
Yes	14	20

Do you play a musical instrument?

a. Of the 2100 students in the school, how many would you expect to play a musical instrument? Justify your answer.

b. Are playing a musical instrument and playing on a sports team independent events? Justify your answer.

c. Estimate the probability that an arbitrary student at the school plays on a sports team and plays a musical instrument. Justify your answer.

d. Estimate the probability that a student who plays on a sports team also plays a musical instrument. Justify your answer.

Sample 3

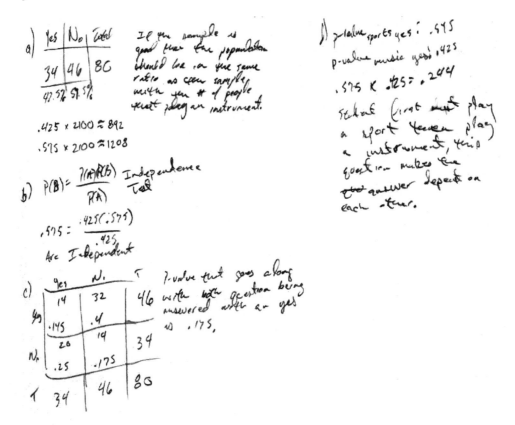

Error: Although a procedural error occurs in part b of this solution, the student appears to have a good conceptual understanding of probability.

Comments: On part a the student finds the correct answer but neglects to label her answers, so which number is the solution is difficult to tell. Her written explanation on part a is appropriate. ("If the sample is good then the population should be in the same ratio as the sample with the number of people that play an instrument.") On part b this student uses the wrong rule for testing for independence. She should have used $P(A|B) = P(A)$ if the two events are independent. The student uses her understanding of the table to reason the answer to part c instead of relying on the probability rules. Because this student has determined these two events to be independent in part b, she uses the rule

$$P(A \text{ and } B) = P(A)\, P(B),$$

which accounts for the error in her solution.

Concluding Thoughts on Error Analysis

Careful analysis of student errors allows the teacher to discover and evaluate both the strengths and the weaknesses of the student's work as a basis for more effective instruction. A comprehensive analysis may include student interviews, which can not only reveal the extent and degree of students' difficulties but, more important, also determine the exact nature of their misunderstandings or misconceptions. This type of diagnostic approach should be regarded as an essential and integral part of regular classroom assessment. The classroom teacher has a responsibility to evaluate students' errors, misunderstandings, or misconceptions and then use this information to revise existing instructional plans or devise new ones designed to enhance students' understanding.

Scoring and Rubrics

Assessment in mathematics serves many purposes. One of the most important is to provide information that contributes to appropriate instructional decisions. Another is to provide a progress report to the student. Providing information for instructional purposes or making decisions regarding student progress must depend on what the evidence tells us about what students know and are able to do. Examining student work is a crucial component in the assessment process. Evidence of student learning is found in student work, and when that work is carefully selected and is linked with specific learning targets, it can become an essential component in raising the standards of student learning. Whether assessment is designed to provide information or to make instructional decisions, it is necessary to develop a form of communication so that both teachers and students can correctly interpret the information that is presented. Evaluation of assessment breaks down into two related but different methods: scoring and grading. Scoring is comparing student work against a standard. This standard could be a description of how points will be allocated for partial credit or simply a determination of whether the answer is right or wrong. Grading is what is done with a set of scores to summarize student performance and communicate it to others. Letter grades, percents, rankings, and descriptive paragraphs are ways to communicate to people outside the classroom how a student has performed.

Common Types of Assessment Items

Multiple Choice

One of the most popular types of assessment is the multiple-choice question. Questions of this type are used in the classroom, in state and districtwide assessments, in college-placement examinations, and in a variety of other situations. Multiple-choice questions are easy to score because the student selects one correct response among a number of choices. Such questions can assess a variety of topics in a relatively short period of time. Well-written multiple-choice questions with good distractors can provide information on the types of errors—arithmetic mistakes, algebraic misconceptions, or procedural errors—made by a student. Short tasks and basic skills can be evaluated easily with multiple-choice questions.

Multiple-choice questions do not give a great deal of information about the student's knowledge of concepts. A student who chooses the correct answer by a process of elimination may have used a sound mathematical strategy or employed a test-taking strategy taught by a coach. We have no way to determine the process that students used to choose their correct answer, and therefore this method does not offer a lot of insight into whether students understand the content being assessed or what algorithms students may have used during the assessment task. For the outcome of the assessment to guide curriculum and instruction, a classroom teacher usually needs more information than a set of multiple-choice questions can provide.

Some teachers modify their use of multiple-choice questions so that students have to do more than simply choose the correct answer. A student may be asked to explain or justify why the answer chosen is correct or why the other responses are incorrect. This approach provides more information about a student's mathematical knowledge but also makes evaluating the task more difficult. Instead of simply giving a point for choosing the correct answer, for example, the teacher may want to assign two points to the task: one for choosing the correct response and one for giving a correct explanation. A multiple-choice question that asks for justification or explanation fosters more insight for the teacher than a more traditional multiple-choice question.

Short Response

Scoring a short-response question can be as simple as determining whether the student's work is right or wrong but usually requires some sort of rubric or scoring map to determine the student's score. For example, a short-response question can be scored on a two-point scale in which two points means that the student has provided a correct answer with correct work; one point means that a student has given a partially correct answer; and zero points indicates that the student has not successfully completed the task, either by being off task or by applying an incorrect algorithm or concept to the assessment. Tests that students have traditionally taken at the end of a unit in their classrooms usually involve a combination of short-response and multiple-choice questions. Several skills and concepts can then be included on one test and scored relatively easily.

Extended Response

The assessment tool that can provide teachers with the most detailed information about what students know and are able to do is the extended-response question. An extended-response item can also help teach new mathematics content by introducing new terms in a context in which a student uses previously learned skills. Since extended responses may vary greatly, a rubric is needed to evaluate students' work. The rubric may be holistic, that is, look at the overall quality of students' performance, or it may be analytic, that is, look at different perspectives or components of students' work. Regardless of the type, students must be told of the scoring scheme and rubric configuration before assessments of any type are given.

Holistic Scoring

An extended-response question that can be solved through several different methods poses a real challenge for a teacher to evaluate. If the question has more than one possible answer, a holistic rubric may be useful to evaluate students' work. Since the overall quality of students' performance is being evaluated, the teacher has no need to assign points to specific parts in the process. The total points in a holistic scoring scale may vary, but points should be assigned on the following characteristics: the answer is clear; the explanation is clear and complete; the explanation includes a mathematically correct reason; if appropriate, a diagram is provided that relates directly and correctly to the information in the problem.

Holistic Scoring Samples

The following models illustrate the use of holistic scoring, first giving the scoring scale and then presenting several samples of the use of that scale.

Scoring Model I

In triangle ABC below, the altitudes BN and CM intersect at point S. The measure of angle MSB is 40°, and the measure of angle SBC is 20°. Write a *proof* of the following statement: "Triangle ABC is isosceles." (See chapter 3, problem 6, for the complete item.)

Rubric for Scoring Model I: 3 Points

Number
of Points   Criteria

3 points   An excellent proof. Provides valid reasons for all statements.
                 Presents statements in logical order. Clearly shows how given
                 information leads to desired conclusion.

2 points   A good proof. Presents statements in a logical order. Uses given
                 information to make desired conclusion but may miss some
                 steps in the process. May also present incorrect or incomplete
                 reasons for proof statements.

1 point   A developing proof. Presents statements in logical order.
                 Attempts to use given information. Does not provide enough
                 statements with valid reasons to complete proof.

0 points   An incomplete proof. Does not present statements in a logical
                 order. Does not use or ineffectively uses given information. Does
                 not provide enough statements with valid reasons to complete
                 proof.

Scoring Model I—Student Work

Score: 1 point
Several statements are incorrect. Reasons are missing or incomplete, and no
logical progression is evident in the proof.

Scoring Model I—Student Work 2

Score: 0 points

This proof is incomplete. The statements and reasons do not match, and the statements do not follow a logical order.

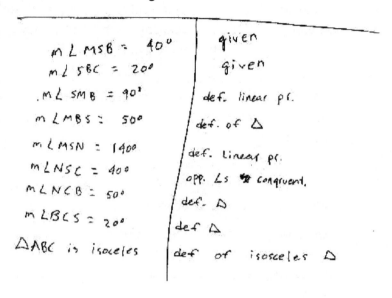

m∠MSB = 40°	given
m∠SBC = 20°	given
.m∠SMB = 90°	def. linear pr.
m∠MBS = 50°	def. of △
m∠MSN = 140°	def. linear pr.
m∠NSC = 40°	opp. ∠s ☷ congruent.
m∠NCB = 50°	def. △
m∠BCS = 20°	def △
△ABC is isoceles	def of isosceles △

Scoring Model I—Student Work 3

Score: 2 points

Incorrect names of angles make communication unclear, although the student seems to make a logical progression through the proof.

Angle MSB is 40° so opposite angles are congruent, making NSC 40° also. If angle N & angle M are both 90° and we know that all complete triangles add up to 180°. So if 2 of the 3 angles equals 130° then the final angles of NSC & MSB is is 50°. Add 50° to the other 20° given for angle B (which is also the same for angle C) b/c the angle measurement for MSB & NSC are all congruent, we know the full measurement of angle C & B is 70%. In an Isosceles triangle, 2 sides must be equal length & in order for them to be equal in length, 2 of the 3 angles must also be congruent. So, since ∠B & ∠C are both 70°, then the triangle ABC is isosceles.

Scoring Model II

In the figure below, $\overline{AB} \parallel \overline{DE}$ and $\overline{DF} \perp \overline{CE}$. Determine the perimeter of $\triangle CDE$. Explain completely how you found your answers and how you know they are correct. (See chapter 3, problem 5, for the complete item.)

Rubric for Scoring Model II: 4 Points

4 points   Correctly uses properties of similar triangles, proportions, and the Pythagorean theorem to determine perimeter

3 points   Uses properties of similar triangles, proportions, and the Pythagorean theorem to determine perimeter but makes arithmetic or algebraic errors

2 points   Attempts to use properties of similar triangles, proportions, and the Pythagorean theorem to determine perimeter but sets up equations or uses formulas incorrectly

1 point   Uses only the Pythagorean theorem or similar triangles but does not continue to determine the correct perimeter

0 points   Gives an incorrect or incomplete response

Scoring Model II—Student Work 1

Score: 2 points

The student uses both similar triangles and the Pythagorean theorem. The distance *EF* is correct, but the distance *CF* is incorrect. The student gets the wrong value for the perimeter because of an error using the Pythagorean theorem. Another error is in naming similar triangles. $\triangle ABC$ is similar to $\triangle DEC$, not $\triangle CDE$.

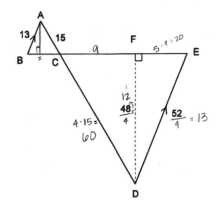

ΔABC ~ ΔCDE and they have a ratio of 1:4. therefore if I multiply the lengths in ΔABC by 4 I would figure out the lengths of ΔCDE. Then I would figure out CD = 60, CF = 9, and EF = 20 because of Pythagorean Triples. So the perimeter of ΔCDE is 102.

Scoring Model II—Student Work 2

Score: 3 points

The student starts with the Pythagorean theorem to find the missing sides of the right triangle. She sets up the ratios correctly, but she never states that the triangles are similar. She states that "the ratios of the sides they are all equal," but this statement is true because she set them up to be equal.

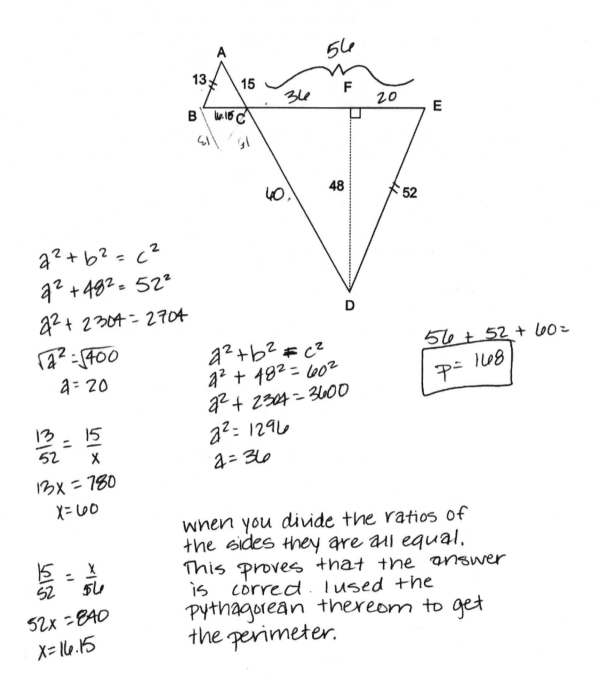

$$a^2 + b^2 = c^2$$
$$a^2 + 48^2 = 52^2$$
$$a^2 + 2304 = 2704$$
$$\sqrt{a^2} = \sqrt{400}$$
$$a = 20$$

$$\frac{13}{52} = \frac{15}{x}$$
$$13x = 780$$
$$x = 60$$

$$\frac{15}{52} = \frac{x}{56}$$
$$52x = 840$$
$$x = 16.15$$

$$a^2 + b^2 = c^2$$
$$a^2 + 48^2 = 60^2$$
$$a^2 + 2304 = 3600$$
$$a^2 = 1296$$
$$a = 36$$

$$56 + 52 + 60 =$$
$$P = 168$$

when you divide the ratios of the sides they are all equal. This proves that the answer is correct. I used the Pythagorean thereom to get the perimeter.

Analytic Scoring Samples

An extended-response question that has several steps to the solution or parts to the problem may be evaluated by a partial credit or analytic scoring scheme. Students earn points for correct steps along the way even if they do not successfully complete the problem and get the correct answer. An instructor may also decide to give points for the process even if an error happens before the student continues to the next step. A student may know what to do mathematically to solve the problem but may make a calculation error that results in an incorrect answer. This type of scoring is more traditional and has been the basis for evaluating most student work in the past.

The following models can be used for analytic scoring; each model gives the problem first, then the scale, and finally several examples illustrating the use of the scoring scale.

Scoring Model III

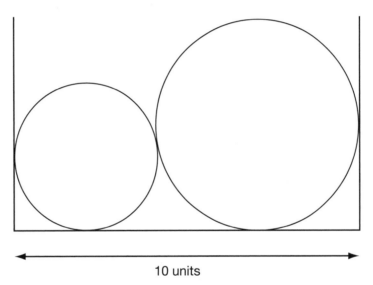

10 units

a. Describe a strategy that you could use to find the radius of the large marble.
b. Use this strategy to calculate the radius of the large marble.

Rubric for Scoring Model III: 4 Points

Number of Points	Criteria
1 point	Describes an appropriate strategy in part (a)
1 point	Sets up a correct equation in part (b)
2 points	Solves the equation
−1 point	Makes an algebra or arithmetic error

Scoring Model III—Student Work 1

Score: 4 points

Whether to award the first point is questionable. Is what the student wrote enough to be called a "strategy"? What if the diagram was not present or was unlabeled? This response presents a good opportunity to discuss how to communicate effectively.

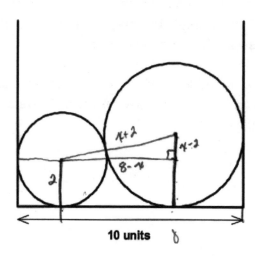

10 units

a. Describe a strategy that you could use to find the radius of the large marble.

Pythagorean thm & solve for x

b. Use this strategy to calculate the radius of the large marble.

$(8-x)^2 + (x-2)^2 = (x+2)^2$

$64 - 16x + x^2 + x^2 - 4x + 4 = x^2 + 4x + 4$

$x^2 - 24x + 64 = 0$

$x = 3.06$

Scoring Model III—Student Work 2

Score: 0 points

The student presents an incorrect strategy. The centers of the marbles are incorrectly placed, because they would not be in a line parallel to the bottom of the container.

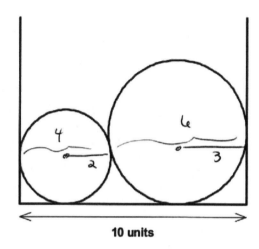

10 units

a. Describe a strategy that you could use to find the radius of the large marble.

Double the radius of the smaller marble to get 4 units. Subtract 4 from the base length to get 6 units for the big marble. Divide 6 by 2 to get the big marbles radius, 3 units.

b. Use this strategy to calculate the radius of the large marble.

3 units

Scoring Model IV

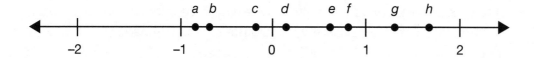

Given the points with coordinates $a, b, c, \ldots, h$ as shown, which point is closest to—

a. ab?

b. $|c|$?

c. $\dfrac{1}{f}$?

d. $\sqrt{e}$?

e. $\sqrt{h}$?

Rubric for Scoring Model IV: 10 Points

Number of Points	Criteria
2 points	1 point: Responds that point *e* is closest to *ab* 1 point: Gives explanation of correct answer
2 points	1 point: Responds that point *d* is closest to |c| 1 point: Gives explanation of correct answer
2 points	1 point: Responds that point *g* is closest to $^1/_f$ 1 point: Gives explanation of correct answer
2 points	1 point: Responds that point *f* is closest to $\sqrt{e}$ 1 point: Gives explanation of correct answer
2 points	1 point: Responds that point *g* is closest to $\sqrt{h}$ 1 point: Gives explanation of correct answer
–1 point	Any of the explanations is based solely on approximating values of variables (deducted only once)

Scoring Model IV—Student Work 1

Score: 9 points

Although the answers are correct, one point is deducted because the only explanation given is based on approximate values of the variables.

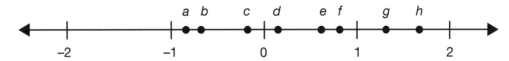

Given the points with coordinates *a, b, c, . . . , h* as shown, which point is closest to—

a. *ab?*   c

b. $|c|$?   d

c. $\dfrac{1}{f}$?   g

d. $\sqrt{e}$?   f

e. $\sqrt{h}$?   g

a: When you multiply the about points of "a" and "b", you would get a positive number close to about e. Point "a" is about -0.9 and point "b" is about -0.8, so when multiplied together, the answer is a positive 0.72, closest to point "c".

b: The absolute value of point "c" is just the exact number but used on the positive side.

c: Putting one over a whole number makes the result smaller but putting one over a decimal makes the result bigger. Point "f" is about 0.9 or ($\frac{9}{10}$) and putting that under one would be the same as multiplying by the reciprocal. $\frac{1}{\frac{9}{10}} = \frac{1}{1} \cdot \frac{10}{9} = \frac{10}{9}$ or $1\frac{1}{9}$ and that is closest to point "g".

d. Taking the square root of a whole number results in a smaller answer whereas taking the square root of a decimal results in a bigger answer. Point "e" is about .9 and the $\sqrt{.9}$ is about .95 so the closest point is "f".

e: The square root of "h" is about $\sqrt{1.9}$ which is about 1.37 and the closest point is g.

187

Scoring Model IV—Student Work 2

Score: 2 points

One point is given for each of the correct answers for parts b and c, but no points are given for their justification.

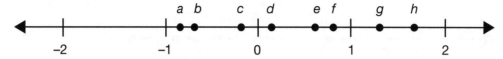

Given the points with coordinates $a, b, c, \ldots, h$ as shown, which point is closest to—

a. ab?   el It is somewhat || similar.

b. $|c|$?   d (it's opposit)

c. $\dfrac{1}{f}$?   g It is close to 1÷.9.

d. $\sqrt{e}$?   e (I guessed by $\sqrt{.5}$)

e. $\sqrt{h}$?   d It was closest to $\sqrt{1.5}$

Scoring Model V

A cat ages faster than a human. To help us understand the age of our cats, cat years are sometimes compared with human years. Here are two models for comparing the age of cats with the age of humans.

Model 1: Each cat year is equivalent to 7 human years.

Model 2: The first year of a cat's life is the same as 15 human years. The second year of a cat's life is equivalent to 10 human years. Each additional cat year is equivalent to 4 human years.

a. Make a chart that compares cat years with human years for each model. Your chart should include at least four years.

b. Write an equation using each model for when the cat is 3 or more years old.

c. Which model has the cat aging faster after the first two years of the cat's life? Explain how you know.

d. Calculate the cat's age in human years if the cat is 10 years old, using both model 1 and model 2. Determine which model gives the greater age for the cat. Show all your work.

e. To the nearest month, how old will the cat be when both models give the cat the same human age? At what age(s) does this outcome occur? Show your work.

Rubric for Scoring Model V: 12 Points

a. 2 points
 	
    1 point: Correctly represents both models
    1 point: Shows at least four years in table							

	Year	1	2	3	4	5	6
	Model 1	7	14	21	28	35	42
	Model 2	15	25	29	33	37	41

b. 2 points
 	
    1 point each: Arrives at correct equations based on student's models
	Model 1: $c = 7h$
	Model 2: $c = 4h + 17$
	Where c represents cat's age and
	  h represents human years.

c. 2 points
 	
    1 point: Gives correct model based on student's work in part (b)
    1 point: Explains answer in slope or rate of change
	Model 1
	Since slope is rate of change, model 1 has the cat aging faster with a slope of 7.

d. 2 points 1 point each: Arrives correct answer based on student's work in part (b)	Model 1: $c = 7(10) = 70$ years Model 2: $c = 4(10) + 17 = 40 + 17 = 57$ years

e. 3 points
 	
    1 point: Sets model 1 equal to model 2
    1 point: Attains correct cat's age based on student's models
    1 point: Gives correct human years based on student's models
	$7h = 4h + 17$
	$3h = 17$
	$h = \frac{17}{3} = 5\frac{2}{3}$
	
	5 years, 8 months in human years
	
	$c = \frac{17}{3}(7) = \frac{119}{3} = 39\frac{2}{3}$

f. 1 point: Includes correct units in parts (d) and (e)	39 years, 8 months in cat's age

Scoring Model V—Student Work 1

a. Make a chart that compares cat years to human years for each model. Your chart should include at least 4 years.

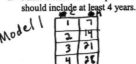

Model 1

C	H
1	7
2	14
3	21
4	28

Model 2

C	H
1	15
2	32
3	36
4	40

b. Write an equation using each model for when the cat is 3 or more years old.

$$Age = 3 + 7h$$

$$Age = 36 + (h-3)4$$

c. Which model has the cat aging faster after the first two years of the cat's life? Explain how you know.

Model 1, because the increments are of 7, not of 4.

d. Calculate the cat's age in human years if the cat is 10 years old using both Model 1 and Model 2. Determine which model gives the greatest age for the cat. Show all of your work.

$$3 + 7(10) = 73$$
LARGER!

$$36 + (10-3)4 =$$
$$36 + 28 = 64$$

e. To the nearest month, how old will the cat be when both models give the cat the same human age? At what human age(s) does this occur? Show your work.

$$3 + 7h = 36 + (10-h)4$$
$$3 + 7h = 36 + 40 - 4h$$
$$11h = 73$$
$$h = \frac{73}{3} \quad \boxed{\approx 24}$$

Score: 7 points

a. *1 point*   Table for second model is incorrect.

b. *1 point*   First equation does not model what is presented in the student work in part a.

c. *2 points*   Even though the word *increments* is used instead of *slope*, the student understands that this number dictates the rate of change.

d. *2 points*   Even though the answers, which the student imported from part b, are incorrect, the method for finding the answers is correct on the basis of the student's previous findings.

e. *1 point*   Student does not earn the last two points owing to the arithmetic error in the work and failure to find the corresponding cat's age.

Units: *0 point*   Units are not included in part d and part e.

Scoring Model V—Student Work 2

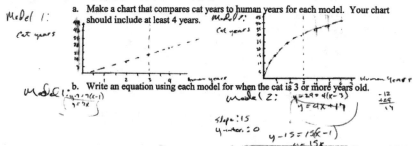

a. Make a chart that compares cat years to human years for each model. Your chart should include at least 4 years.

b. Write an equation using each model for when the cat is 3 or more years old.

c. Which model has the cat aging faster after the first two years of the cat's life? Explain how you know.

d. Calculate the cat's age in human years if the cat is 10 years old using both Model 1 and Model 2. Determine which model gives the greatest age for the cat. Show all of your work.

e. To the nearest month, how old will the cat be when both models give the cat the same human age? At what human age(s) does this occur? Show your work.

Score: 10 points

a. *2 points*	The word *chart* is sometimes used to refer to graphs as well as tables. The teacher should clarify to students what terminology is acceptable here.
b. *2 points*	Two equations seem to have been drawn for the second model, but since the box highlights the first one, it is assumed to be the student's answer.
c. *2 points*	Correct answer is attained. Since slopes can be seen from the student's equation, the values of the slopes do not have to be repeated here.
d. *0 points*	Incorrect substitutions are made in model 1, and the wrong equation is used in model 2.
e. *3 points*	Correct answer is attained.
Units: *1 point*	Response addresses units in last two parts.

Scoring Model V—Student Work 3

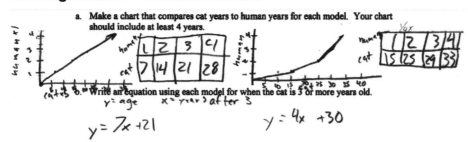

a. Make a chart that compares cat years to human years for each model. Your chart should include at least 4 years.

	1	2	3	4
cat	7	14	21	28

y/ax	1	2	3	4
cat	15	25	29	33

b. Write an equation using each model for when the cat is 3 or more years old.

y = age   x = years after 3

$$y = 7x + 21$$

$$y = 4x + 30$$

c. Which model has the cat aging faster after the first two years of the cat's life? Explain how you know.

2nd, graphs indicate/after 2 years in the 1st, a cat is 14 yrs old in the 2nd model, the cat is 25 yrs old

d. Calculate the cat's age in human years if the cat is 10 years old using both Model 1 and Model 2. Determine which model gives the greatest age for the cat. Show all of your work.

Model 1 $y = 7x$ $10 = 7x$ $x = \frac{10}{7}$

Model 2 $y = 15x$ $10 = 15x$ $x = \frac{2}{3}$

Model 1

e. To the nearest month, how old will the cat be when both models give the cat the same human age? At what human age(s) does this occur? Show your work.

$$x - 2 = \frac{1}{4}(x - 25)$$
$$y - 2 = \frac{1}{4}x - \frac{25}{4}$$
$$x = \frac{1}{4}x - \frac{17}{4}$$

$$y = \frac{1}{7}x$$

$$\frac{1}{7}x = \frac{1}{4}x - \frac{17}{4}$$
$$-\frac{3}{28}x = \frac{17}{4}$$
$$x = \frac{119}{3}$$

$$\frac{119}{3} = 7x$$
human years $= \frac{17}{3}$ yrs
5 yrs 8 months/August

cat 39 yrs 8 months/August

Score: 5 Points

a. *2 points*   Correct answer is attained.

b. *0 points*   Neither equation correctly models the situation for years 3 or more.

c. *0 points*   Answer is based on what happens in second year.

d. *0 points*   The models presented in part b are not used to answer part d.

e. *3 points*   Even though the equations from part b are not used, the equations found are correctly based on the data in part a.

Units: *0 points*   Units are not present in part d.

Scoring Model VI

Bill is on a hiking trip, where he hikes to the top of a large cliff (121 meters high) and accidentally drops his backpack off the edge. Sue is at the bottom of the cliff 43 meters from the base of the cliff. She sees what is happening and tries to catch the backpack. She runs toward the base of the cliff as fast as she can at the exact moment the backpack is dropped. After 1 second she is 35 meters away from the base.

a. Model Sue's distance from the base of the cliff as a linear function of the time she has been running. Identify what each variable in the function represents.

b. Use your model to predict how long Sue will take to reach the base of the cliff. Show your work.

c. After 1 second Bill's backpack is approximately 116 meters above the base of the cliff. After 2 seconds Bill's backpack is approximately 101 meters above the base of the cliff. Write a quadratic function that models the fall of Bill's backpack. Show your work, or explain your method.

d. Use your function from part c to predict how long Bill's backpack will take to reach the base of the cliff. Show your work.

e. Can Sue get to the base of the cliff in time to catch Bill's backpack? Justify your answer.

Rubric for Scoring Model VI: 12 Points

a.	2 points
	    1 point: Gives correct equation
	    1 point: Defines variables
		$d = 43 - 8t$
		d is distance in meters
		t is time in seconds

b.	2 points
	    1 point: Sets equation in part a equal to 0
	    1 point: Correctly solves equation
		$43 - 8t = 0$
		$43 = 8t$
		$\frac{43}{8} = t$
		
		Sue will reach the base of the cliff in 5.375 seconds.

c.	3 points
	    2 points: Substitutes the given ordered pairs in a quadratic equation
	    1 point: Gives correct equation
		vertex (0, 121); passes through (1, 116)
		$$y = a(t-0)^2 + 121$$
		$$116 = a(1)^2 + 121$$
		$$-5 = a$$
		$$y = -5(t-0)^2 + 121$$
		$$y = -5t^2 + 121$$
		y is the distance above the ground
		t is the time in seconds

d.	2 points
	    1 point: Sets equation from part c equal to zero
	    1 point: Attains correct solution to equation
	    {Note: 0 points in this section if the equation is not quadratic}
		$$-5t^2 + 121 = 0$$
		$$121 = 5t^2$$
		$$\frac{121}{5} = t^2$$
		$$t = \sqrt{\frac{121}{5}} \approx 4.919$$
		
		Bill's backpack will take approximately 4.919 seconds to reach the base of the cliff.

e.	2 points
	    1 point: Answer is correct on the basis of student's results in part b and part d
	    1 point: Gives explanation of correct answer
		No.
		    Sue takes 5.375 seconds to reach the bottom of the cliff, but the backpack will reach the ground in 4.919 seconds.

f.	1 point: Uses correct units throughout problem	Units

Scoring Model VI—Student Work 1

a. Model Sue's distance from the base of the cliff as a linear function of the time she has been running. Identify what each variable in the function represents.

Sue 10/s

$D = 43 - 10x$

D - distance ~~Sue has traveled~~ from cliff
x - time in seconds
43 - distance to cliff
10x - distance Sue has traveled

b. Use your model to predict how long it will take Sue to reach the base of the cliff. Show your work.

$0 = 43 - 10x$
$-43 = -10x$
$x = \frac{43}{10}$ seconds = 43 seconds

in regular quadratic, chart goes (0,0)(1,1) (2,4)(3,9)...
The y value was multiplied by five in problem, thus the equation is multiplied by 5.

c. After 1 second Bill's backpack is approximately 116 meters above the base of the cliff. After 2 seconds Bill's backpack is approximately 101 meters above the base of the cliff. Write a quadratic function that models the fall of Bill's backpack. Show your work or explain your method.

0,0   1,5   2,20

$y = -5x^2 + 121$

y = distance from ground
x = seconds from drop
121 = height of cliff
$-5x^2$ = distance backpack has traveled

d. Use your function from part c to predict how long it will take Bill's backpack to reach the base of the cliff. Show your work.

$0 = -5x^2 + 121$
$-121 = -5x^2$
$24.2 = x^2$
$x = 4.92$ seconds

e. Can Sue get to the base of the cliff in time to catch Bill's backpack? Justify your answer.

yes, the time it takes Sue to get to the cliff is less than the time it takes the backpack to fall.

Score: 8 points

a. *1 point*   Gives incorrect equation

b. *1 point*   Correctly sets equation from part a equal to 0 but makes arithmetic error

c. *1 point*   Does not adequately show how given information leads to equation

d. *2 points*   Attains correct solution

e. *2 points*   Gives correct answer on the basis of solutions to parts b and d

Units: *1 point*   Includes units in each section as appropriate

Scoring Model VI—Student Work 2

a. Model Sue's distance from the base of the cliff as a linear function of the time she has been running. Identify what each variable in the function represents.

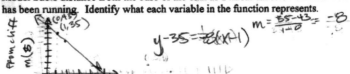

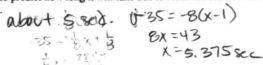

b. Use your model to predict how long it will take Sue to reach the base of the cliff. Show your work.

about 5 sec. $y-35 = -8(x-1)$

$-35 = -\frac{1}{8}x + \frac{1}{8}$ $8x = 43$

$\frac{1}{5} = 28$ $x = 5.375$ sec

c. After 1 second Bill's backpack is approximately 116 meters above the base of the cliff. After 2 seconds Bill's backpack is approximately 101 meters above the base of the cliff. Write a quadratic function that models the fall of Bill's backpack. Show your work or explain your method.

$(2, 101)$ $y - 101 = -15(x - 2)$
$(1, 116)$

$m = \dfrac{116 - 101}{1 - 2}$

$= -15$

d. Use your function from part c to predict how long it will take Bill's backpack to reach the base of the cliff. Show your work.

$0 - 101 = -15(x - 2)$

$15x = 131$

$x = 8.733$ sec.

e. Can Sue get to the base of the cliff in time to catch Bill's backpack? Justify your answer.

Yes, she can reach the cliff in 5.4 sec, & Bill's backpack will reach it in 8.7 sec.

Score: 6 points

a. *1 point*   Presents equation in point-slope form; does not define variables (some might consider them implied from the points on the graph)

b. *2 points*   Correctly sets *y* equal to 0 and solves for *x*

c. *0 points*   Uses points in linear function but uses no quadratic function

d. *0 points*   Gives linear but not quadratic equation

e. *2 points*   Attains correct answer on the basis of the work in part b and part d

Units: *1 point*   Uses units throughout problem

Scoring Model VII

A star is made by cutting quarter circles from a square sheet of cardboard with sides of length L, as shown.

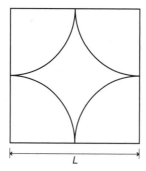

a. Write an expression for the area of the star as a function of side length L.
b. About what fraction of the area of the square was cut away to make the star?
c. Does the answer to part b depend on the length of L? Explain.
d. How far could a bug walk along the edge of the star, without retracing its path, before returning to its starting point?
e. Does the answer to part d depend on the length of L? Explain.

Rubric for Scoring Model VII: 7 Points

a. *1 point* *1 point:* Correctly expresses the area as a function of side length	$A(L) = L^2 - \pi\left(\dfrac{1}{2}L\right)^2$ $= L^2 - \dfrac{1}{4}\pi L^2$
b. *1 point* *1 point:* Gives correct fraction	$\dfrac{1}{4}\pi \approx 0.785$
c. *2 points* *1 point:* Answers correctly *1 point:* Gives explanation for correct answer	No. The ratio of the areas is $\dfrac{\pi\left(\dfrac{1}{2}L\right)^2}{L^2} = \dfrac{\dfrac{1}{4}\pi L^2}{L^2} = \dfrac{1}{4}\pi.$ The amount cut away will always be $\dfrac{1}{4}\pi$. Since π is a constant, the length of L does not matter.
d. *1 point:* States length in terms of L	$2\pi\left(\dfrac{1}{2}L\right) = \pi L$
e. *2 points* *1 point:* Answers correctly *1 point:* Gives explanation for correct answer	Yes. When calculating πL, as L gets larger, the distance the bug walks becomes longer.

Scoring Model VII—Student Work 1

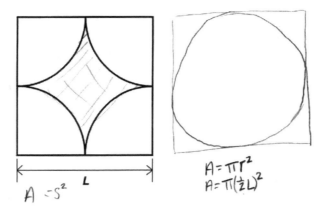

$A = s^2$ L

$A = \pi r^2$
$A = \pi(\frac{1}{2}L)^2$

a. Write an expression for the area of the star as a function of side length L.

$A = L^2 - \left(\pi \frac{L}{2}\right)^2$

b. About what fraction of the area of the square was cut away in order to make the star?

$\frac{4}{5}$

c. Does the answer to part b depend upon the length L? Explain.

No because in order to create the stars then the sides of the quarters circles need to touch making them bigger in proportion to the square.

d. How far could a bug walk along the edge of the star, without retracing its path, before returning to its starting point?

$C = 2\pi r$
$C = 2\pi\left(\frac{L}{2}\right)$

e. Does the answer to part d depend upon the length L? Explain.

yes because if length L is larger then the bug would have to walk farther to get around the circle.

Score: *4 points*

a. *0 points*   Incorrectly uses π in parentheses.

b. *1 point*   Arrives at acceptable answer on the basis of the question asked: "About what fraction …?"

c. *1 point*   Gives correct answer but incomplete explanation

d. *1 point*   Gives correct answer, albeit not in simplified form

e. *1 point*   Gives correct answer but should refer to the solution to part d in the explanation

Scoring Model VII—Student Work 2

a. Write an expression for the area of the star as a function of side length L.

$2 \cdot L - \frac{3}{4} \pi (\frac{1}{2}L)^2 =$ area of star or square - area of ⊙ with radius of ½L

b. About what fraction of the area of the square was cut away in order to make the star?

$$\frac{\text{area of star}}{\text{area of square}}$$

c. Does the answer to part b depend upon the length L? Explain.

NO. due to the fact that the prop. will stay the same no matter the length of L.

d. How far could a bug walk along the edge of the star, without retracing its path, before returning to its starting point?

πr^2 or the circumference of the ⊙ with the radius of ½·L

e. Does the answer to part d depend upon the length L? Explain.

Yes. due to the fact that the circumference, or should say each quarter of its circumference, is proportional to the length of L.

Score: 3 points

a. *0 points*   Gives incorrect equation

b. *0 points*   Gives incomplete response

c. *1 point*   Gives correct answer but incomplete explanation

d. *0 points*   Gives incorrect answer

e. *2 points*   Gives correct answer but should refer to the solution to part d in the explanation

General Comments on Scoring

The reader may or may not agree with us on the scoring of these problems. An important part of using rubrics is finding one that fits your style of teaching and your assessment methods, then sharing it with your students up front. Your rubric may be different from those of other teachers, but that variation is fine as long as your students understand your expectations and are taught accordingly. Also important is being consistent in the way in which the rubric is applied.

Other Types of Assessment

Portfolios, projects, and other types of assessment involve more complex scoring because no single process or answer is involved when these types of assessment are used. Portfolios give an overview of a student's progress over time but cause real problems in deciding how to evaluate that progress. Rubrics constructed to evaluate projects can be holistic or analytic, depending on what information the teacher seeks to gain from the assessment. The more information gathered from the particular assessment, the more in-depth and comprehensive the proper assessment tool will be. Teachers should choose these tools carefully and think through their evaluation before actually giving them to students.

A very instructional approach for students and teachers alike is to involve students in the development of rubrics and in the scoring process. Students who actually become part of the scoring process are able to better understand what is expected of them and how they can structure their own responses to show evidence of their mathematical proficiency.

Blackline Masters

Number and Operations

Name _____   Date _____

1. List these numbers in increasing order: 2^{800}, 3^{600}, 5^{400}, 6^{200}

Smallest _____

Second _____

Third _____

Largest _____

How did you decide?

Number and Operations

Name _____   Date _____

2. What is the units digit of 3^{1992}? Write a convincing mathematical argument that supports your solution.

Number and Operations

Name _____   Date _____

3. Given the expression $1! + 2! + \cdots + 205!$, what is the units digit of the sum? Clearly communicate your reasoning, and explain how you know that your response is mathematically correct.

Number and Operations

Name _____   Date _____

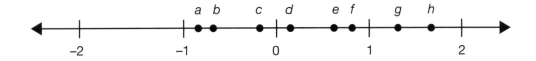

4. Given the points with coordinates *a, b, c, ..., h* as shown, which point is closest to—

    a. *ab?*

    b. $|c|$?

    c. $\dfrac{1}{f}$?

    d. $\sqrt{e}$?

    e. $\sqrt{h}$?

Source: Adapted from *Principles and Standards for School Mathematics* (NCTM 2000, p. 293, fig. 7.1)

Number and Operations

Name _____   Date _____

5. An examination consists of thirteen questions. A student must answer only one of the first two questions and only nine of the remaining ones. How many choices of questions does the student have?

    a. $_{13}C_{10} = 286$

    b. $_{11}C_8 = 165$

    c. $2 \times {}_{11}C_9 = 110$

    d. $2 \times {}_{11}P_2 = 220$

    e.   none of the above

Source: TIMSS Population 3 Item Pool (L-4)

Number and Operations

Name _____   Date _____

6. In how many ways can one arrange on a bookshelf 5 thick books,
    4 medium-sized books, and 3 thin books so that the books of the same
    size remain together?

    a. 5! 4! 3! 3! = 103,680

    b. 5! 4! 3! = 17,280

    c. (5! 4! 3!) $\times$ 3 = 51,840

    d. 5 $\times$ 4 $\times$ 3 $\times$ 3 = 180

    e. $2^{12} \times 3 = 12,288$

Source: TIMSS Population 3 Item Pool (K-2)

Number and Operations

Name _____   Date _____

7. While working on a problem, Christine observed that $_5P_1$ and $_5C_1$ give the same value but that the value for $_5P_2$ is larger than the value for $_5C_2$. Explain why this outcome occurs.

Source: Adapted from Nova Scotia Department of Education (2002). All rights reserved. Used with permission.

Number and Operations

Name _____   Date _____

Challenger

8. You are the Keeper of the Digits 0, 1, 2, 3, 4, 5, 6, 7, 8, and 9. On the way to school this morning, you lost the digit 9. What happens to our base ten number line as a result of the loss of the digit 9?

Number and Operations

Name _____   Date _____

Challenger

9. Mersenne primes are of the special form

    $$M_p = 2^p - 1,$$

    where p is another prime.

    (Not all values of p give primes. $M_2 = 3$, $M_3 = 7$, $M_5 = 31$, $M_7 = 127$, but $M_{11} = 2047$, which is not prime.) How many digits are in the Mersenne prime $M_{24,036,583}$?

Algebra

Name _____   Date _____

1. The price of a particular product doubles every 35 years. If the price of the product was $16.50 on January 1, 1996, then the price of the product will be $36.50 in what year?

   a. 2028

   b. 2031

   c. 2036

   d. 2040

   Justify your answer.

Source: Adapted from Nova Scotia Department of Education (2002). All rights reserved. Used with permission.

Algebra

Name _____   Date _____

2. If $xy = 1$ and x is greater than 0, which of the following statements is true? Show the work that justifies your answer.

    a.   When x is greater than 1, y is negative.

    b.   When x is greater than 1, y is greater than 1.

    c.   When x is less than 1, y is less than 1.

    d.   As x increases, y increases.

    e.   As x increases, y decreases.

Source: TIMSS Population 3 Item Pool (K-1)

Algebra

Name _____   Date _____

3. In February 2000 the cost of sending a letter by first-class mail was
    33 cents for the first ounce and an additional 22 cents for each additional
    ounce or portion thereof through 13 ounces. Choose the graph that best
    represents the cost of mailing a letter that weighs 4 ounces or less.

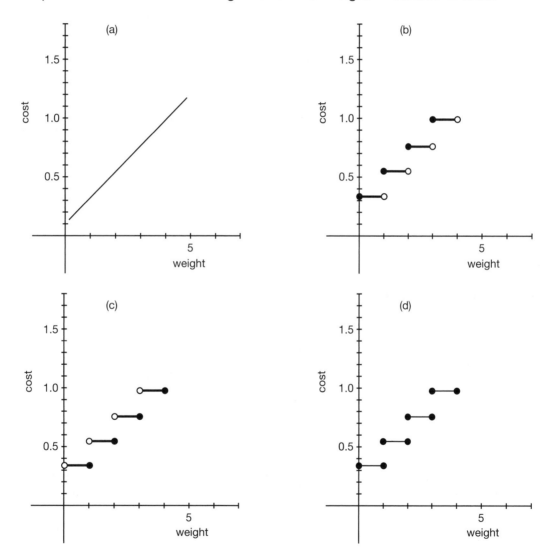

Source: Adapted from *Principles and Standards for School Mathematics* (NCTM 2000, p. 298, fig. 7.4)

Algebra

Name _____   Date _____

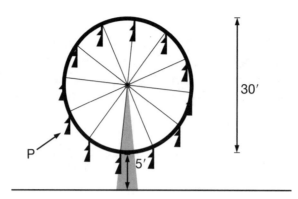

4. The Ferris wheel above is 30 feet in diameter and 5 feet above the ground. It turns at a steady rate of one revolution each 30 seconds. The graph that follows shows the distance from the ground of a person (P) as a function of time if the person is at the top of the Ferris wheel at time 0.

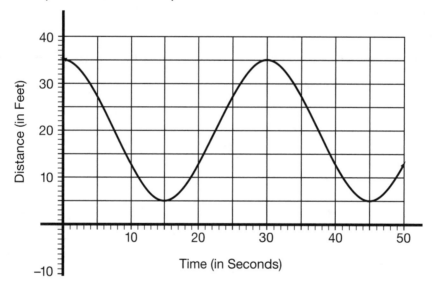

On the same graph draw a second curve that shows a person's distance from the ground, as a function of time, if that person is at the <u>bottom</u> of the Ferris wheel at time 0 and if the Ferris wheel turns at a steady rate of one revolution each <u>15</u> seconds.

Source: Adapted from *Results from the Seventh Mathematics Assessment of the National Assessment of Educational Progress* (Silver and Kenney 2000)

Algebra

Name _____ Date _____

5. A cat ages faster than a human. To help us understand the age of our cats, cat years are sometimes compared with human years. Here are two models for comparing the age of cats with the age of humans.

    Model 1: Each cat year is equivalent to 7 human years.

    Model 2: The first year of a cat's life is the same as 15 human years. The second year of a cat's life is equivalent to 10 human years. Each additional cat year is equivalent to 4 human years.

    a. Make a chart that compares cat years with human years for each model. Your chart should include at least four years.

    b. Write an equation using each model for when the cat is 3 or more years old.

    c. Which model has the cat aging faster after the first two years of the cat's life? Explain how you know.

    d. Calculate the cat's age in human years if the cat is 10 years old, using both model 1 and model 2. Determine which model gives the greatest age for the cat. Show all your work.

    e. To the nearest month, how old will the cat be when both models give the cat the same human age? At what human age(s) does this outcome occur? Show your work.

Source: Adapted from *Big Sky STARS: Student and Teacher Assessment Resources* (Montana Council of Teachers of Mathematics 2003). All rights reserved. Used with permission.

Algebra

Name _____   Date _____

6. Bill is on a hiking trip, where he hikes to the top of a large cliff (121 meters high) and accidentally drops his backpack off the edge. Sue is at the bottom of the cliff 43 meters from the base of the cliff. She sees what is happening and tries to catch the backpack. She runs toward the base of the cliff as fast as she can at the exact moment the backpack is dropped. After 1 second she is 35 meters away from the base.

   a. Model Sue's distance from the base of the cliff as a linear function of the time she has been running. Identify what each variable in the function represents.

   b. Use your model to predict how long Sue will take to reach the base of the cliff. Show your work.

   c. After 1 second Bill's backpack is approximately 116 meters above the base of the cliff. After 2 seconds Bill's backpack is approximately 101 meters above the base of the cliff. Write a quadratic function that models the fall of Bill's backpack. Show your work, or explain your method.

   d. Use your function from part c to predict how long Bill's backpack will take to reach the base of the cliff. Show your work.

   e. Can Sue get to the base of the cliff in time to catch Bill's backpack? Justify your answer.

Source: Adapted from *Big Sky STARS: Student and Teacher Assessment Resources* (Montana Council of Teachers of Mathematics 2003). All rights reserved. Used with permission.

Algebra

Name _____   Date _____

7.   Upon taking his first job, Stuart Martin is given one of the following three options for his retirement plan.

Option A: $0.05 the first year

$0.15 the second year

$0.45 the third year

For every year following, triple the amount of the previous year.

Option B: $10 the first year

$20 the second year

$40 the third year

For every year following, double the amount of the previous year.

Option C: $100,000 the first year

$200,000 the second year

$300,000 the third year

For every year following, add $100,000 to the previous year's amount.

Your job is to give Stuart advice about which option is best. Using mathematics, show him which option is best for the short term and for the long term.

Source: Adapted from Oregon Department of Education (www.ode.state.or.us/asmt/mathematics)

Algebra

Name _____   Date _____

8. When trying to weigh some goods, a shopkeeper found that his balance scale was slightly bent, with one arm of the scale longer than the other. He was not worried until a customer ordered two pounds of nuts, which unfortunately were not packaged. The shopkeeper stated that he would take a one-pound weight and put it on the right side of the scale and balance it on the left with nuts. He then stated he would put the same one-pound weight on the left side of the scale and balance it on the right with nuts. He told the customer that he was sure that together the two packages would weigh more than two pounds.

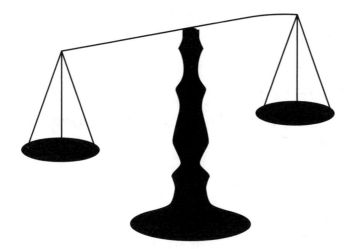

Would you advise the customer to accept the deal? Explain using mathematical language how you reached your conclusion.

Algebra

Name _____   Date _____

9. On the first day of school Lise's teacher asks the students what 1 + 1
   equals, and the students reply 2. The next day the teacher asks what 2 + 2
   equals, and the students reply 4. The next day the teacher asks what 4 + 3
   equals, and the students reply 7. The teacher continues this questioning on
   each day of school by taking the sum from the previous day and adding
   the day of school to yield the following pattern:

Sum from Previous Day		Day in the School Year		Sum
1	+	1	=	2
2	+	2	=	4
4	+	3	=	7
7	+	4	=	11
11	+	5	=	16

If the school year has 180 school days, what will be the sum on the last
day of school?

Algebra

Name _____   Date _____

10. Given the following pinball arrangement, how many different paths can a ball travel from the top to the bottom? A move can be made only to a spot diagonally adjacent and below. We start at row 0 because our first move takes us to the next row.

If this pattern continues to row 15, how many different paths will result? Write a general rule for calculating the number of possible paths, p, in relation to the number of rows, r.

Algebra

Name _____ Date _____

11. For each of the following, sketch the graph of a function—

    a. that always increases and is never negative;

    b. whose graph lies in exactly two quadrants;

    c. that is quadratic and whose graph lies in exactly three quadrants;

    d. having both positive and negative values that are never greater than 1 or smaller than –1;

    e. that looks exactly the same when shifted to the right (by any amount);

    f. that is quadratic and never intersects the *x*-axis;

    g. that looks the same when reflected in a mirror that lies along the *y*-axis.

Source: Adapted from *Balanced Assessment for the 21st Century* (Schwartz and Kenney 2000, p. 129, problem HC011). These tasks were developed with the support of the National Science Foundation. Copyright © 1995–2000 by President and Fellows of Maryland College. All rights reserved. Used with permission.

Algebra

Name _____   Date _____

12. For each of the following, write a symbolic expression (i.e., a formula) for a function—

   a.   that always increases and is never negative;

   b.   whose graph lies in exactly two adjacent quadrants;

   c.   whose graph lies in exactly two nonadjacent quadrants;

   d.   whose graph lies in exactly three quadrants;

   e.   that is quadratic and whose graph lies in exactly two quadrants;

   f.   that is quadratic and whose graph lies in exactly three quadrants;

   g.   that is quadratic and whose graph lies in all four quadrants;

   h.   that has a graph that looks like the letter V.

Source: Adapted from *Balanced Assessment for the 21st Century* (Schwartz and Kenney 2000, p. 129, problem HC011). These tasks were developed with the support of the National Science Foundation. Copyright © 1995–2000 by President and Fellows of Maryland College. All rights reserved. Used with permission.

Algebra

Name _____   Date _____

13. If a certain medicine is absorbed by your body at a rate so that 1/3 of the original amount is left after 8 hours and if your doctor gives you 10 grams today and does not want more than 10 grams to accumulate in your system, how much medicine should she give you tomorrow at the same time?

Algebra

Name _____   Date _____

14. A gardener plants tomatoes in a square pattern. To protect the tomatoes from insects, she surrounds the tomatoes with marigolds. The diagram below shows the pattern of tomato plants and marigolds for any number (*n*) of rows of tomato plants. Find the number of marigolds on the basis of the number of tomato plants.

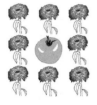
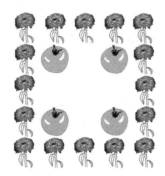
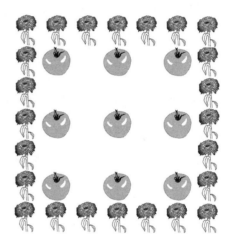

Algebra

Name _____   Date _____

15. The population of the world was 3.9 billion in 1970 and 6.3 billion in 2000. If the rate of growth is assumed proportional to the number present, what estimate would you give for the population in 2020? Some researchers estimate that the earth can sustain a maximum population of 50 billion. If the population growth continues at the same rate, when will the earth's population reach 50 billion?

Algebra

Name _____   Date _____

16. Bill's house is 5 miles east-northeast of town, and Sue's house is due east of town on Highway 63. A straight dirt road from Bill's house to Sue's house is 7 miles long. What angle does the dirt road make with Highway 63?

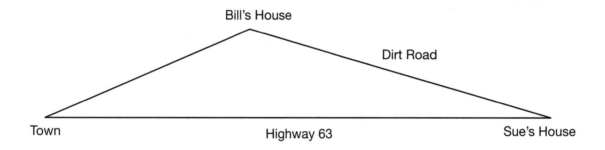

Algebra

Name _____ Date _____

17. Designs for the locations of communications towers, aerial tramways, ski lifts, and air lanes all depend on establishing the equation of a line of sight. Suppose that a section of the Rocky Mountains has the skyline described by the graph of

$$y = -x^4 - 2x^3 + 12x^2 + x - 10$$

for $-4 < x < 3$. Find an equation that represents the line of sight that just grazes the two mountain peaks.

Source: Adapted from *Contemporary College Algebra* (Small 2003, p. 53). All rights reserved. Used with permission.

Algebra

Name _____ Date _____

18. When an earthquake occurs, energy waves radiate in concentric circles from the epicenter, the point above where the earthquake occurred. Stations with seismographs record the level of that energy and the length of time the energy took to reach the station.

    a. Suppose that one station determines that the epicenter of an earthquake is about 200 miles from the station. Find an equation for the possible location of the epicenter.

    b. A second station, 120 miles east and 160 miles north of the first station, shows the epicenter to be about 235 miles away. Find an equation for the possible location of the epicenter.

    c. Using the information from parts a and b, find the possible locations of the epicenter.

Source: Adapted from *Enhancing Teacher Quality: Algebra II* (Charles A. Dana Center 2005, task 7.4.2). This item was developed with support (in part) from the Texas Higher Education Coordinating Board. All rights reserved. Used with permission.

Geometry

Name _____   Date _____

1. $\overline{AB}$ is the diameter of a semicircle k, C is an arbitrary point on the semi-
    circle (other than A or B), and S is the center of the circle inscribed in
    triangle ABC.

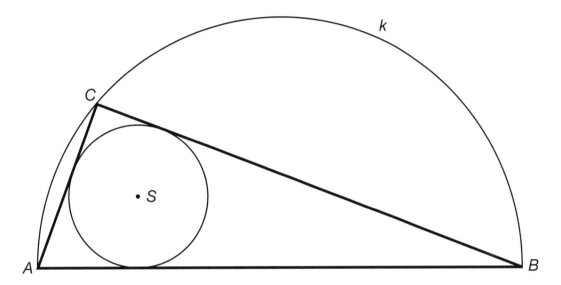

Which of the following must be true?

a. The measure of angle ASB changes as C moves on k.

b. The measure of angle ASB is the same for all positions of C, but it
    cannot be determined without knowing the radius.

c. The measure of angle ASB is 135° for all C.

d. The measure of angle ASB is 150° for all C.

Justify your answer.

Source: Adapted from TIMSS Population 3 Item Pool (K-10)

Geometry

Name _____   Date _____

2. The vertices of the triangle *PQR* are the points *P*(1, 2), *Q*(4, 6), and *R*(–4, 12). Which one of the following statements about triangle *PQR* must be true?

    a. *PQR* is a right triangle with the right angle at *P*.

    b. *PQR* is a right triangle with the right angle at *Q*.

    c. *PQR* is a right triangle with the right angle at *R*.

    d. *PQR* is not a right triangle.

    Justify your answer.

Source: TIMSS Population 3 Item Pool (K-7)

Geometry

Name _____   Date _____

3. The rectangular coordinates of three points in a plane are $Q(-3, -1)$,
    $R(-2, 3)$, and $S(1, -3)$. A fourth point T is chosen so that vector ST is
    equal to twice vector QR. The y-coordinate of T is _____.

    a. −11

    b. −7

    c. −1

    d. 1

    e. 5

    Show how you got your answer.

Source: TIMSS Population 3 Item Pool (L-8)

Geometry

Name _____   Date _____

4. A ship travels due south for 40 miles and then southwest for 30 miles.
    Which of the vectors in the figure below best represents the result of the
    ship's movement from its starting point? Justify your answer.

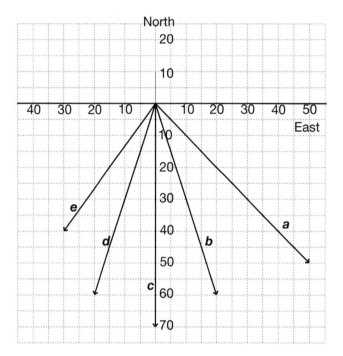

Source: Adapted from *Results from the Seventh Mathematics Assessment of the National Assessment of Educational
Progress* (Silver and Kenney 2000)

Geometry

Name _____ Date _____

5. In the figure below, $\overline{AB} \parallel \overline{DE}$ and $\overline{DF} \perp \overline{CE}$. Determine the perimeter of
△*CDE*. Explain completely how you found your answers and how you
know they are correct.

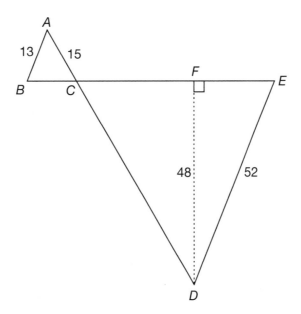

Source: *Principles and Standards for School Mathematics* (NCTM 2000, p. 310, fig. 7.12)

Geometry

Name _____   Date _____

6. In triangle *ABC* below, the altitudes *BN* and *CM* intersect at point *S*. The measure of angle *MSB* is 40°, and the measure of angle *SBC* is 20°. Write a *proof* of the following statement: "Triangle *ABC* is isosceles."

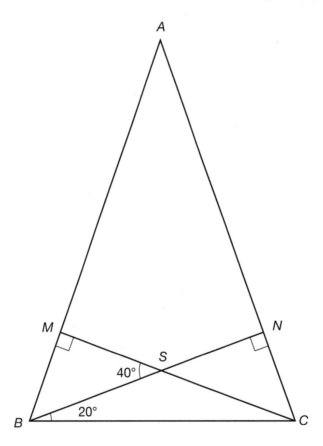

Source: Adapted from TIMSS Population 3 Item Pool (K-18)

Geometry

Name _____   Date _____

7. Consider a triangle *ABC* with vertices *A*(–5, 1), *B*(–4, 7), and *C*(–8, 5). Reflect the triangle over the line *y* = *x* to obtain the triangle *A'B'C'*, as shown below.

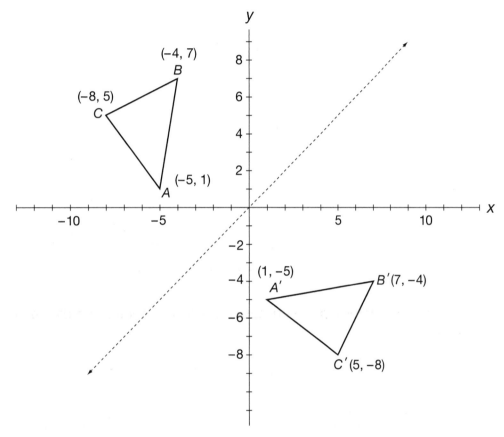

Determine a matrix *M* such that *MA* = *A'*, *MB* = *B'*, and *MC* = *C'*.

Source: *Principles and Standards for School Mathematics* (NCTM 2000, p. 315, fig. 7.17)

Geometry

Name _____   Date _____

8. Two marbles are sitting side by side in a glass container. The base of the container is 10 units in length, and the radius of the smaller marble is 2 units.

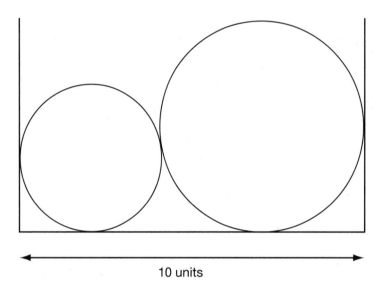

10 units

a. Describe a strategy that you could use to find the radius of the large marble.

b. Use this strategy to calculate the radius of the large marble.

Source: *Balanced Assessment for the Mathematics Curriculum* (Schwartz and Kenney 2000, p. 37, BA 18-02, HS074). These tasks were developed with the support of the National Science Foundation. Copyright © 1995–2000 by President and Fellows of Maryland College. All rights reserved. Used with permission.

Geometry

Name _____   Date _____

9. A star is made by cutting quarter circles from a square sheet of cardboard with sides of length *L*, as shown.

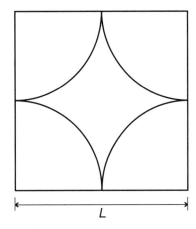

a. Write an expression for the area of the star as a function of side length *L*.

b. About what fraction of the area of the square was cut away to make the star?

c. Does the answer to part b depend on the length *L*? Explain.

d. How far could a bug walk along the edge of the star, without retracing its path, before returning to its starting point?

e. Does the answer to part d depend on the length *L*? Explain.

Source: Adapted from *Balanced Assessment for the Mathematics Curriculum* (Schwartz and Kenney 2000, p. 29, BA 18-02, problem HS034). These tasks were developed with the support of the National Science Foundation. Copyright © 1995–2000 by President and Fellows of Maryland College. All rights reserved. Used with permission.

Geometry

Name _____   Date _____

10. The diameter of the given circle is the same length as the side of the given square. For each of the shapes below, use your geometry tools to construct a figure that has exactly the same shape and whose—

    a.   perimeter/circumference is twice as long.

    b.   area is twice as large.

    In each instance, explain your reasoning.

Source: Adapted from *Balanced Assessment for the 21st Century* (Schwartz and Kenney 2000, p. 93, problem HS012). These tasks were developed with the support of the National Science Foundation. Copyright © 1995-2000 by President and Fellows of Maryland College. All rights reserved. Used with permission.

Geometry

Name _____   Date _____

11. Use the grid below to answer the questions. Show as much of your work as possible. Sketch a smaller square inside the given square so that the smaller square is half the area of the larger square. Write an explanation to convince another person that your new, smaller square is truly half the area of the original square.

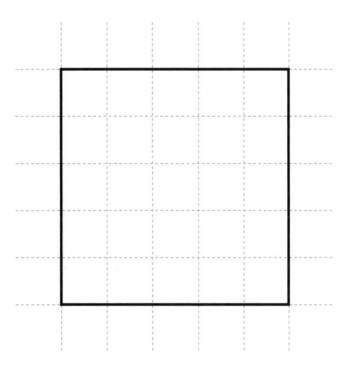

Geometry

Name _____   Date _____

12. The dimensions of a small house are 12 meters long, 12 meters wide, and 3 meters tall. The roof forms a pyramid with all edges measuring 12 meters. An extra room is needed, so your job is to design an attic room, inscribed in the pyramid, that has the same length, width, and height.

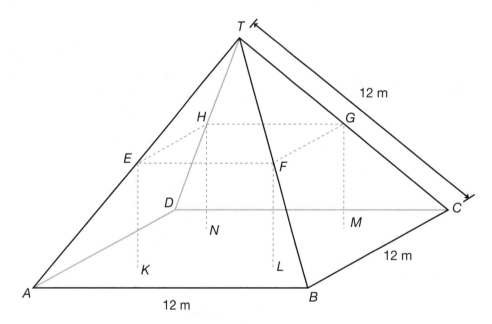

a.   What are the length, width, and height of the room you designed?

b.   Is the attic room taller or shorter than the downstairs rooms?

c.   Do these dimensions seem appropriate for a room, or should the plan be revised? Explain your response.

d.   The space behind the four walls of the new room can be used as storage. What is the volume of this storage space?

Source: Adapted from *Preparing Students for PISA: Mathematical Literacy* (Nova Scotia Department of Education 2002, p. 23). All rights reserved. Used with permission.

Geometry

Name _____   Date _____

Challenger

13. What is the geometric probability that two positive numbers, *x* and *y* (both less than 1), written down at random, together with the number 1, yield a trio of numbers (*x*, *y*, 1) that are the sides of an obtuse-angled triangle?

Source: *Ingenuity in Mathematics* (Honsberger 1970, p. 4). All rights reserved. Used with permission.

Measurement

Name _____   Date _____

1. You are headed to Canada, and you need to know how many hours the drive from Calgary, Alberta, to Edmonton, Alberta, will take. The only distance you are able to find between these two cities is 294 kilometers.

   a. If speed limits in Canada are comparable to speed limits in the United States and you usually average 60 miles per hour when traveling, how many hours will the trip take?

   b. Your car averages 26 miles per gallon. How many liters of fuel will you need for the trip? (Fuel in Canada is sold in liters.)

   c. Fuel prices in the United States are approximately $2.75 per gallon in comparison with fuel prices in Canada, which are approximately $1.04 Canadian dollars per liter. United States prices are given in United States dollars, and Canadian prices are given in Canadian dollars. Where would it cost less to travel the 294 kilometers, the United States or Canada?

   Conversions you may need for this problem
   are the following:

   1 kilometer = .6214 miles

   1 gallon = 3.785 liters

   1 U. S. dollar = 1.3264 Canadian dollars

Measurement

Name _____ Date _____

2. The diameter of the given circle is the same length as the side of the given square. For each of the shapes below, use your geometry tools and construct a figure that has exactly the same shape and whose—

    a. perimeter/circumference is twice as long.

    b. area is twice as large.

    In each instance, explain your reasoning.

Source: Adapted from *Balanced Assessment for the 21st Century* (Schwartz and Kenney 2000, p. 93, problem HS033). These tasks were developed with the support of the National Science Foundation. Copyright © 1995–2000 by President and Fellows of Maryland College. All rights reserved. Used with permission.

Measurement

Name _____   Date _____

3. A star is made by cutting quarter circles from a square sheet of cardboard with sides of length *L,* as shown.

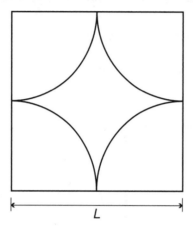

a. Write an expression for the area of the star as a function of side length *L*.

b. About what fraction of the area of the square was cut away to make the star?

c. Does the answer to part b depend on length *L*? Explain.

d. How far could a bug walk along the edge of the star, without retracing its path, before returning to its starting point?

e. Does the answer to part d depend on length *L*? Explain.

Source: Balanced *Assessment for the Mathematics Curriculum* (2002, BA 18-02, p. 29, problem HS034). These tasks were developed with the support of the National Science Foundation. Copyright © 1995–2000 by President and Fellows of Maryland College. All rights reserved. Used with permission.

Measurement

Name _____   Date _____

4. Use the grid below to answer the questions. Show as much of your work
    as possible. Sketch a smaller square inside the given square so that the
    smaller square is half the area of the larger square. Write an explanation to
    convince another person that your new, smaller square is truly half the area
    of the original square.

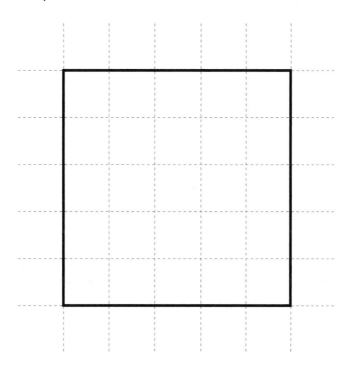

Measurement

Name _____   Date _____

5. The dimensions of a small house are 12 meters long, 12 meters wide, and 3 meters tall. The roof forms a pyramid with all edges measuring 12 meters. An extra room is needed, so your job is to design an attic room, inscribed in the pyramid, that has the same length, width, and height.

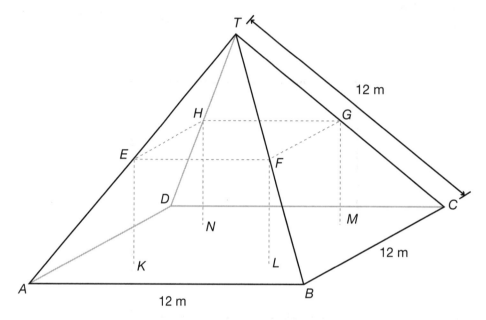

a. What are the length, width, and height of the room you designed?

b. Is the height of the attic room larger or smaller than that of the down-stairs rooms?

c. Do these dimensions seem appropriate for a room, or should the plan be revised? Explain your response.

d. The space behind the four walls of the new room can be used as storage. What is the volume of this storage space?

Measurement

Name _____   Date _____

6. Albert ran across the following graph that showed the variable luminosity of a galactic body observed over a period of several days. He noted that the variability was approximately linear when the time, or horizontal, axis was scaled logarithmically.

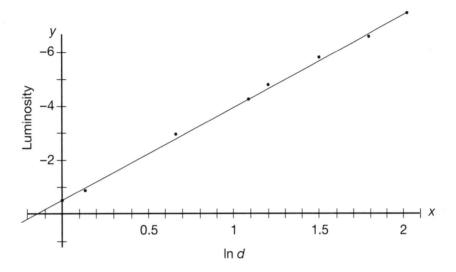

a. At approximately what time, in days (d), would the luminosity be −3?

b. If $y = -3.6x - 0.5$ is the equation of the line predicting luminosity, what is the predicted luminosity after 14 days?

Note: For this type of application, physicists often orient the y-axis so that the negative direction is up and the positive is down. Thus, the line in the graph has a negative slope.

Data Analysis and Probability

Name _____   Date _____

1. A warning system installation consists of two independent alarms having probabilities of operating in an emergency of 0.95 and 0.90, respectively. Find the probability that at least one alarm operates in an emergency. Show your work.

    a.   0.995

    b.   0.975

    c.   0.95

    d.   0.90

    e.   0.855

    Source: TIMSS Population 3 Item Pool (L-10)

Data Analysis and Probability

Name _____   Date _____

2. If the population increases by the same average rate from the year 1990 to
    the year 2005 as in the years from 1975 to 1985, approximately what is the
    expected population by the year 2005? Justify your answer.

    a. 47 million

    b. 50 million

    c. 53 million

    d. 58 million

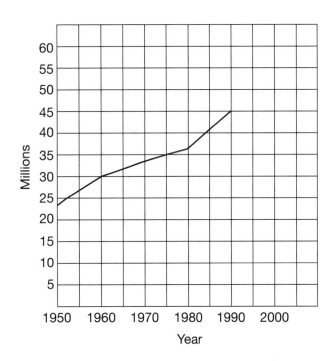

Source: Adapted from TIMSS Population 3 Item Pool (A-4)

Data Analysis and Probability

Name _____   Date _____

3. Scientists have observed that crickets move their wings faster in warm temperatures than in cold temperatures. By noting the pitch of cricket chirps, one can estimate the air temperature. Below is a graph showing thirteen observations of cricket chirps per second and the associated air temperature.

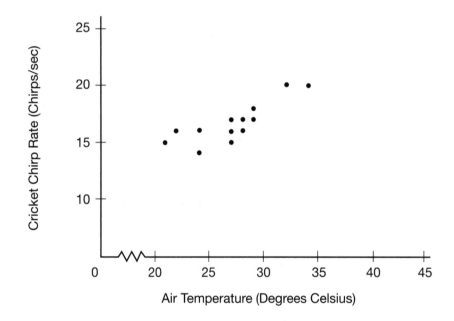

a. On the graph, draw in an estimated line of best fit for these data.

b. Using your line, estimate the number of cricket chirps per second when the air temperature is 30 degrees Celsius.

Source: Adapted from TIMSS Population 3 Item Pool (L-15a)

Data Analysis and Probability

Name _____   Date _____

4.   The diagram below shows the results of a two-question survey adminis-
     tered to 80 randomly selected students at Highcrest High School.

Do you play on a
sports team?

		Yes	No
Do you play a musical instrument?	No	32	14
	Yes	14	20

a.   Of the 2100 students in the school, how many would you expect to
     play a musical instrument? Justify your answer.

b.   Are playing a musical instrument and playing on a sports team inde-
     pendent events? Justify your answer.

c.   Estimate the probability that an arbitrary student at the school plays on
     a sports team and plays a musical instrument. Justify your answer.

d.   Estimate the probability that a student who plays on a sports team
     also plays a musical instrument. Justify your answer.

Source: Adapted from *Principles and Standards for School Mathematics* (NCTM 2000, pp. 331–32)

Data Analysis and Probability

Name _____   Date _____

5. Twenty-five people watched a movie showing at Empire Theaters. Of them, fifteen order a drink, eight order popcorn, and seven order candy. Two people order all three items, three order drink and candy, five order drink and popcorn, and three order popcorn and candy.

    a. Display the results in a Venn diagram.

    b. What is the probability that a moviegoer who buys a drink will also buy popcorn?

Data Analysis and Probability

Name _____ Date _____

6. The following data set compares the average number of hours studied per week with a student's GPA.

Hours Studied	12	8	2	6	10	5	10	9	3	4
GPA	3.97	3.20	2.15	2.95	3.45	2.86	3.75	3.05	2.45	2.20

   a. Graph the data, and find a line of best fit.

   b. Add a point that would not change the slope of the line of best fit but would increase the *y*-intercept when *y* represents the GPA and *x* represents "hours studied."

   c. Add a point that would increase the slope of the line of best fit.

Data Analysis and Probability

Name _____   Date _____

7. A class of 350 graduating seniors found their heights to be approximately normally distributed, with a mean of 68 inches and a standard deviation of 3 inches.

    a. Draw the normal distribution, labeling the mean and ±3 standard deviations from the mean.

    b. How many students' heights lie between 1 and 2 standard deviations above the mean? How do you know?

    c. How many students' heights fall less than 2 standard deviations below the mean? How do you know?

Data Analysis and Probability

Name _____   Date _____

8.   The following data set is a list of scores on Mrs. Davis's third-period geom-
     etry test: 20, 56, 96, 84, 84, 83, 91, 70, 74, 88, 64, 67, 63, 84, 88, 84, 70,
     73, 75, 71, 84, 90, 85, 87, 84.

     a.   Draw a box-and-whiskers plot of the data.

     b.   Describe the center, shape, and spread.

     c.   If Mrs. Davis were to discuss the results with her class, what important
          observations might she make about the data?

Data Analysis and Probability

Name _____   Date _____

Challenger

9.   What is the geometric probability that two positive numbers, x and y (both less than 1), written down at random, together with the number 1, yield a trio of numbers $(x, y, 1)$ that are the sides of an obtuse-angled triangle?

Source: Adapted from *Ingenuity in Mathematics* (Honsberger 1970, p. 4). All rights reserved. Used with permission.

Appendix
Items Matrices

Number and Operations Items Matrix, Chapter 1

Assessment Item Number	1	2	3	4	5	6	7	8	9
Standards and Expectations									
Understand numbers, ways of representing numbers, relationships among numbers, and number systems									
Develop a deeper understanding of very large and very small numbers and of various representations of them	X	X	X						X
Compare and contrast the properties of numbers and number systems, including the rational and real numbers								X	
Understand meanings of operations and how they relate to one another									
Judge the effects of such operations as multiplication, division, and computing powers and roots on the magnitudes of quantities				X					
Develop an understanding of permutation and combinations as counting techniques					X	X	X		
Process Standards									
Problem Solving			X				X	X	X
Communication	X	X	X	X				X	X
Reasoning and Proof		X	X	X			X	X	X
Connections								X	
Representation				X			X		
Item Format (MC = multiple choice; SR = short response; ER = extended response)	SR	SR	SR	SR	MC	MC	SR	ER	ER

Algebra Items Matrix, Chapter 2

Assessment Item Number	1	2	3	4	5	6	7	8	9
Standards and Expectations									
Understand patterns, relations, and functions									
Understand relations and functions and select and use various representations for them				X					
Understand and compare the properties of classes of functions, including periodic functions				X					
Generalize patterns using explicitly defined and recursively defined functions									X
Represent and analyze mathematical situations and structures using algebraic symbols									
Understand the meaning of equivalent forms of expressions, equations, inequalities, and relations		X							
Use symbolic algebra to represent and explain mathematical relationships						X		X	
Use mathematical models to represent and understand quantitative relationships									
Identify essential quantitative relationships in a situation and determine the class or classes of functions that might model the relationship	X		X		X	X	X		X
Use symbolic expressions to represent relationships arising from various contexts					X	X	X		X
Draw reasonable conclusions about a situation being modeled	X					X	X		X
Analyze change in various contexts									
Approximate and interpret rates of change from graphical data				X					
Process Standards									
Problem Solving						X	X	X	X
Communication					X	X	X	X	X
Reasoning and Proof		X						X	
Connections	X		X	X		X	X		X
Representation	X		X	X	X	X	X		X
Item Format (MC = multiple choice; SR = short response; ER = extended response)	MC	MC	MC	SR	ER	ER	ER	SR	SR

Algebra Items Matrix, Chapter 2—Continued

Assessment Item Number	10	11	12	13	14	15	16	17	18
Standards and Expectations									
Understand patterns, relations, and functions									
Generalize patterns using explicitly defined and recursively defined functions	X								
Analyze functions of one variable by investigating rates of change						X		X	
Represent and analyze mathematical situations and structures using algebraic symbols									
Use symbolic algebra to represent and explain mathematical relationships		X	X	X	X	X		X	
Judge the meaning, utility, and reasonableness of the results of symbol manipulations, including those carried out by technology				X				X	
Use mathematical models to represent and understand quantitative relationships									
Identify essential quantitative relationships in a situation and determine the class or classes of functions that might model the relationship							X		X
Use symbolic expressions to represent relationships arising from various contexts				X	X	X			X
Draw reasonable conclusions about a situation being modeled				X			X		X
Analyze change in various contexts									
Approximate and interpret rates of change from graphical data					X	X			
Process Standards									
Problem Solving	X		X	X	X	X	X	X	X
Communication			X	X		X			
Reasoning and Proof	X			X	X	X			
Connections		X	X	X		X	X	X	X
Representation	X	X	X		X		X	X	X
Item Format (MC = multiple choice; SR = short response; ER = extended response)	SR	ER	ER	SR	SR	ER	SR	SR	SR

Geometry Items Matrix, Chapter 3

Assessment Item Number	1	2	3	4	5	6	7	8	9*	10*	11*	12*	13**
Standards and Expectations													
Analyze characteristics and properties of two- and three-dimensional geometric shapes and develop mathematical arguments about geometric relationships													
Analyze properties and determine attributes of two- and three-dimensional objects	X	X			X			X	X				
Explore relationships (including congruence and similarity) of two- and three-dimensional objects and solve problems involving them	X				X			X			X	X	X
Establish the validity of geometric conjectures using deduction, prove theorems, and critique arguments made by others						X							
Specify locations and describe spatial relationships using coordinate geometry and other representational systems													
Use Cartesian coordinates and other coordinate systems to analyze geometric situations		X	X	X						X			
Investigate conjectures and solve problems involving two- and three-dimensional objects represented with Cartesian coordinates			X										
Apply transformations and use symmetry to analyze mathematical situations													
Understand and represent translations, reflections, rotations, and dilations of objects in the plane by using sketches, coordinates, vectors, function notation, and matrices							X						
Use visualization, spatial reasoning, and geometric modeling to solve problems													
Draw and construct representations of two- and three-dimensional geometric objects using a variety of tools										X			
Visualize three-dimensional objects from different perspectives and analyze their cross-sections												X	
Process Standards													
Problem Solving	X						X	X		X	X	X	X
Communication	X	X		X	X	X		X	X	X	X	X	
Reasoning and Proof	X	X			X	X					X	X	
Connections		X					X	X	X	X	X	X	
Representation				X					X	X	X	X	X
Item Format (MC = multiple choice; SR = short response; ER = extended response)	MC	MC	MC	SR	ER	ER	SR	ER	ER	ER	ER	ER	ER

* Item also listed in Measurement   ** Item also listed in Data Analysis and Probability

Measurement Items Matrix, Chapter 4

Assessment Item Number	1	2*	3*	4*	5*	6
Standards and Expectations						
Understand measurable attributes of objects and the units, systems, and processes of measurement						
Make decisions about units and scales that are appropriate for problem situations involving measurement	X			X		X
Apply appropriate techniques, tools, and formulas to determine measurements						
Understand and use formulas for the area, surface area, and volume of geometric figures		X	X	X	X	
Use unit analysis to check measurement computations	X					
Process Standards						
Problem Solving	X	X	X	X	X	X
Communication		X	X	X	X	
Reasoning and Proof				X		
Connections	X	X		X	X	X
Representation		X	X		X	X
Item Format (MC = multiple choice; SR = short response; ER = extended response)	ER	ER	ER	ER	ER	SR

* Items also listed in Geometry

Data Analysis and Probability Items Matrix, Chapter 5

Assessment Item Number	1	2	3	4	5	6	7	8	9**
Standards and Expectations									
Select and use appropriate statistical methods to analyze data									
For univariate measurement data, be able to display the distribution, describe its shape, and select and calculate summary statistics							X	X	
For bivariate measurement data, be able to display the distribution, describe its shape, and determine regression coefficients, regression equations, and correlation coefficients using technological tools						X			
Identify trends in bivariate data and find functions that model the data or transform the data so that they can be modeled						X			
Develop and evaluate inferences and predictions that are based on data									
Understand how sample statistics reflect the values of population parameters and use sampling distributions as the basis for informal inference		X	X						
Understand and apply basic concepts of probability									
Understand the concepts of sample space and probability distribution and construct sample spaces and distributions in simple cases									X
Understand the concepts of conditional probability and independent events	X			X	X				
Understand how to compute the probability of a compound event	X			X	X				
Process Standards									
Problem Solving						X		X	X
Communication				X			X	X	
Reasoning and Proof						X			
Connections				X		X	X	X	
Representation		X	X				X	X	X
Item Format (MC = multiple choice; SR = short response; ER = extended response)	MC	MC	SR	SR	SR	SR	SR	ER	ER

** Item also listed in Geometry

Bibliography

Balanced Mathematics Assessment for the Mathematics Curriculum. BA 18-02. Cambridge, Mass.: Harvard Graduate School of Education, 2002.

Bright, George W., and Jeane M. Joyner. *Dynamic Classroom Assessment: Linking Mathematical Understanding to Instruction in Middle Grades and High School.* Vernon Hills, Ill.: EtaCuisenaire, 2004.

Bush, William S., ed. *Mathematics Assessment: Cases and Discussion Questions for Grades 6–12.* Reston, Va.: National Council of Teachers of Mathematics, 2000.

Bush, William S., and Anja S. Greer, eds. *Mathematics Assessment: A Practical Handbook for Grades 9–12.* Reston, Va.: National Council of Teachers of Mathematics, 1999.

Charles A. Dana Center. *Supporting and Strengthening Standards-Based Mathematics Teacher Preparation: Guidelines for Mathematics and Mathematics Education Faculty.* Austin, Tex.: Charles A. Dana Center, University of Texas at Austin, 2004.

National Council of Teachers of Mathematics (NCTM). *Curriculum and Evaluation Standards for School Mathematics.* Reston, Va.: NCTM, 1989.

———. *Principles and Standards for School Mathematics.* Reston, Va.: NCTM, 2000.

Pellegrino, James W., Robert Glaser, and Naomi Chudowsky, eds. *Knowing What Students Know: The Science and Design of Educational Assessment.* Washington, D.C.: National Academy Press, 2001.

Schwartz, Judah, and Joan Kenney. *Balanced Mathematics Assessment for the 21st Century.* Cambridge, Mass.: Harvard Graduate School of Education, 2000.

Stenmark, Jean Kerr, ed. *Mathematics Assessment: Myths, Models, Good Questions, and Practical Suggestions.* Reston, Va.: National Council of Teachers of Mathematics, 1991.

Wilson, Linda Dager, and Patricia Ann Kenney. "Classroom and Large-Scale Assessment." In *A Research Companion to "Principles and Standards for School Mathematics,"* edited by Jeremy Kilpatrick, W. Gary Martin, and Deborah Schifter, pp. 53–67. Reston, Va.: National Council of Teachers of Mathematics, 2003.

Sources for Assessment Items

Balanced Mathematics Assessment for the Mathematics Curriculum. BA 18-02. Cambridge, Mass: Harvard Graduate School of Education, 2002.

Big Sky STARS: Student/Teacher Assessment Resources. Missoula: Montana Council of Teachers of Mathematics, 2003.

Charles A. Dana Center. *Enhancing Teacher Quality: Algebra II.* Austin, Tex.: Charles A. Dana Center, University of Texas at Austin, 2004.

Honsberger, Ross. *Ingenuity in Mathematics.* Washington, D.C.: Mathematical Association of America, 1970.

Massachusetts Department of Education. http://www.doe.mass.edu/mcas/1998/release/ (accessed January 4, 2005).

National Council of Teachers of Mathematics (NCTM). *Principles and Standards for School Mathematics.* Reston, Va.: NCTM, 2000.

Nova Scotia Department of Education. *Preparing Students for PISA: Mathematical Literacy.* Teacher's Handbook. Halifax: Nova Scotia Department of Education, 2002.

Ore, Oystein. *Invitation to Number Theory,* Washington, D.C.: Mathematical Association of America, 1967.

Oregon Department of Education. Mathematics Assessments. www.ode.state.or.us/asmt/mathematics (accessed January 26, 2005).

Schwartz, Judah, and Joan Kenney. *Balanced Mathematics Assessment for the 21st Century.* Cambridge, Mass.: Harvard Graduate School of Education, 2000.

Silver, Edward A., and Patricia Kenney, eds. *Results from the Seventh Mathematics Assessment of the National Assessment of Educational Progress.* Reston, Va.: National Council of Teachers of Mathematics, 2000.

Small, Don. *College Algebra: Data, Functions, Modeling.* 5th ed. Columbus, Ohio: McGraw Hill Custom Publishing, 2003.

Third International Mathematics and Science Study United States. Michigan State University. ustimss.msu.edu (accessed October 22, 2004).

Three additional titles
are planned for the
Mathematics Assessment Samplers series

Anne M. Collins, series editor

✪ *Mathematics Assessment Sampler, Prekindergarten–Grade 2: Items Aligned with NCTM's* Principles and Standards for School Mathematics,
edited by DeAnn Huinker

✪ *Mathematics Assessment Sampler, Grades 3–5, Items Aligned with NCTM's* Principles and Standards for School Mathematics,
edited by Jane D. Gawronski

✪ *Mathematics Assessment Sampler, Grades 6–8, Items Aligned with NCTM's* Principles and Standards for School Mathematics,
edited by John Burrill

Please consult www.nctm.org/catalog for the availability of these titles, as well as for a plethora of resources for teachers of mathematics at all grade levels.

For the most up-to-date listing of NCTM resources on topics of interest to mathematics educators, as well as information on membership benefits, conferences, and workshops, visit the NCTM Web site at www.nctm.org.